WORLD OF ANIMALS

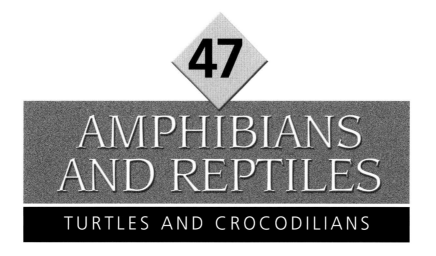

47

AMPHIBIANS AND REPTILES

TURTLES AND CROCODILIANS

Marine Turtles, Freshwater Turtles, Tortoises,
Alligators, Crocodiles ...

DAVID ALDERTON

GROLIER

an imprint of

■SCHOLASTIC

www.scholastic.com/librarypublishing

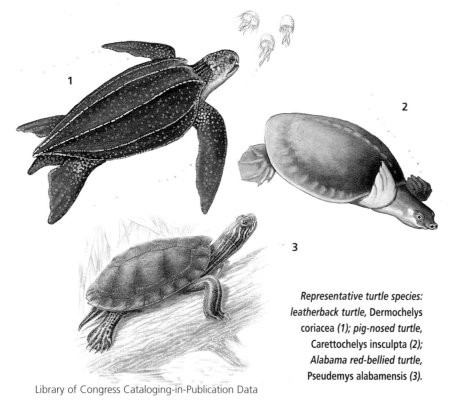

*Representative turtle species:
leatherback turtle, Dermochelys
coriacea (1); pig-nosed turtle,
Carettochelys insculpta (2);
Alabama red-bellied turtle,
Pseudemys alabamensis (3).*

Published 2005 by Grolier, an imprint of
Scholastic Library Publishing
Danbury, CT 06816

This edition published exclusively for the school
and library market

The Brown Reference Group plc.
(incorporating Andromeda Oxford Limited)
8 Chapel Place
Rivington Street
London
EC2A 3DQ

© 2005 The Brown Reference Group plc.

Library of Congress Cataloging-in-Publication Data

Amphibians and Reptiles.
    p. cm. -- (World of Animals; v. 41-50)
    Contents: [1] Salamanders, newts, and caecilians / Chris Mattison -- [2] Frogs and
toads 1 / Chris Mattison -- [3] Frogs and toads 2 / Chris Mattison -- [4] Lizards 1 /
Valerie Davies, Chris Mattison -- [5] Lizards 2 / Chris Mattison -- [6] Lizards 3 / Valerie
Davies, Chris Mattison -- [7] Turtles and crocodilians / David Alderton -- [8] Snakes 1 /
Chris Mattison -- [9] Snakes 2 / Chris Mattison -- [10] Snakes 3 / Chris Mattison.
    ISBN 0-7172-5916-1 (set : alk. paper) -- ISBN 0-7172-5917-X (v. 1 : alk. paper) --
ISBN 0-7172-5918-8 (v. 2 : alk. paper) -- ISBN 0-7172-5919-6 (v. 3 : alk. paper) -- ISBN
0-7172-5920-X (v. 4 : alk. paper) -- ISBN 0-7172-5921-8 (v. 5 : alk. paper) -- ISBN 0-
7172-5922-6 (v. 6 : alk. paper) -- ISBN 0-7172-5923-4 (v. 7 : alk. paper) -- ISBN 0-7172-
5924-2 (v. 8 : alk. paper) -- ISBN 0-7172-5925-0 (v. 9 : alk. paper) -- ISBN 0-7172-5926-
9 (v. 10 : alk. paper)
    1. Amphibians -- Juvenile literature. 2. Reptiles -- Juvenile literature [1. Amphibians. 2.
Reptiles.] I. Grolier (Firm) II. Series: World of Animals (Danbury, Conn.); v. 41-50.
QL49.W877 2003
590--dc22   2002073860

Project Directors:	Graham Bateman, Lindsey Lowe
Editors:	Virginia Carter, Angela Davies
Art Editor and Designer:	Steve McCurdy
Picture Manager:	Becky Cox
Picture Researcher:	Alison Floyd
Main Artists:	Denys Ovenden, Philip Hood, Myke Taylor, Ken Oliver, Michael Woods, David M. Dennis
Maps:	Steve McCurdy, Tim Williams
Production:	Alastair Gourlay, Maggie Copeland

Printed in Singapore

Set ISBN 0-7172-5916-1

About This Volume

The ancestors of the ancient reptilian groups of turtles and crocodilians were present on earth well before the age of the dinosaurs. They survived the major upheaval that drew this era to a close some 65 million years ago and have changed relatively little in terms of their physical appearance since then. The greatest diversity among turtles and crocodilians can be seen in the tropics, but representatives of both groups range more widely—the distribution of turtles extends from Canada in the north to Chile and Argentina at the southern tip of the American continent.

Like their ancestors, turtles and crocodiles can be found in the world's oceans. Turtles have also successfully made the transition to land, and tortoises are even found in arid areas of the world, for example, close to the Sahara Desert in Africa. The largest of all tortoises are found not on the mainland continents, however, but on isolated islands, such as the Galápagos off the northwestern coast of South America.

Misconceptions abound about crocodiles. Although they are reputed to be dangerous killers, only a minority of species represent a potential threat to humans. Studies have revealed the strong maternal instincts prevalent in this group of reptiles, which results in females not only guarding their nest sites, but also caring for the young after hatching. Crocodilians can have a natural life span equivalent to our own, while tortoises are probably the longest lived of all vertebrates, with a possible life span approaching 200 years.

Contents

The oblong snake-necked turtle, Chelodina oblonga, is one of about eight species of turtles with very long necks that cannot be retracted beneath the carapace.

The snapping turtle, Chelydra serpentina, is a large, powerful predator found in many parts of North and Central America.

A known man-eater, the saltwater crocodile, Crocodylus porosus, is the most widely distributed crocodilian.

How to Use This Set

World of Animals: Amphibians and Reptiles is a 10-volume set that describes in detail reptiles and amphibians from all corners of the earth. Each volume brings together those animals that are most closely related and have similar lifestyles. So all the frogs and toads are in Volumes 42 and 43, the snakes are in Volumes 48, 49, and 50, and so on. To help you find volumes that interest you, look at pages 6 and 7 (Find the Animal). A brief introduction to each volume is also given on page 2 (About This Volume).

Article Styles

Each volume contains two types of article. The first kind introduces major groups (such as amphibians, reptiles, frogs and toads, or lizards). It presents a general overview of the subject.

The second type of article makes up most of each volume. It describes in detail individual species, such as the American bullfrog or the American alligator, or groups of very similar animals, such as reed frogs or day geckos. Each article starts with a fact-filled **data panel** to help you gather information at a glance. Used together, the two different styles of article will enable you to become familiar with animals in the context of their evolutionary history and biological relationships.

Data panel presents basic statistics of each animal

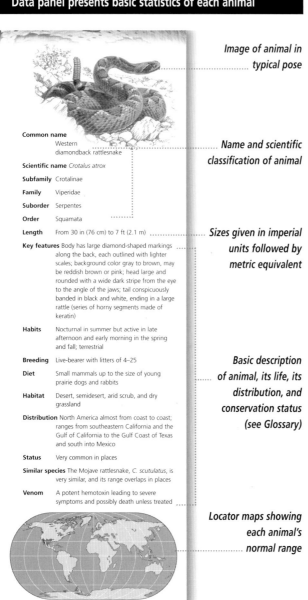

Image of animal in typical pose

Common name
Western diamondback rattlesnake

Name and scientific classification of animal

Scientific name *Crotalus atrox*

Subfamily Crotalinae

Family Viperidae

Suborder Serpentes

Order Squamata

Length From 30 in (76 cm) to 7 ft (2.1 m)

Sizes given in imperial units followed by metric equivalent

Key features Body has large diamond-shaped markings along the back, each outlined with lighter scales; background color gray to brown, may be reddish brown or pink; head large and rounded with a wide dark stripe from the eye to the angle of the jaws; tail conspicuously banded in black and white, ending in a large rattle (series of horny segments made of keratin)

Habits Nocturnal in summer but active in late afternoon and early morning in the spring and fall; terrestrial

Breeding Live-bearer with litters of 4–25

Diet Small mammals up to the size of young prairie dogs and rabbits

Habitat Desert, semidesert, arid scrub, and dry grassland

Distribution North America almost from coast to coast; ranges from southeastern California and the Gulf of California to the Gulf Coast of Texas and south into Mexico

Status Very common in places

Similar species The Mojave rattlesnake, *C. scutulatus*, is very similar, and its range overlaps in places

Venom A potent hemotoxin leading to severe symptoms and possibly death unless treated

Basic description of animal, its life, its distribution, and conservation status (see Glossary)

Locator maps showing each animal's normal range

Article describes a particular animal

Scientific name of animal

Common name of animal

FROGS AND TOADS

Common European Treefrog

Hyla arborea

The treefrogs commonly seen near water throughout most of continental Europe belong to the Hyla arborea complex of species. They are prolific breeders with loud, raucous calls.

Common name Common European treefrog (green tree frog)

Scientific name *Hyla arborea*

Subfamily Hylinae

Family Hylidae

Order Anura

Size From 1.25 in (3 cm) to 2 in (5 cm)

Key features Body plump, color usually bright green, although individuals can change color; there is nearly always a dark line running through the eye; dark line continues onto the flanks, an extension of the line projects upward at an angle just above the groin; toes have well-developed pads

Habits Mainly nocturnal but diurnal on humid or rainy days; arboreal

Breeding Throughout the summer in shallow water; female lays clutches of 200–1,400 eggs; eggs hatch after 14–21 days

Diet Insects, especially flies

Habitat Heavily vegetated areas near water, such as reed beds, hedges, bushes, and trees

Distribution Throughout most of Europe except the British Isles, parts of southern France, southern and eastern Iberia; also into Asiatic Turkey and through the former Soviet states as far as the Caspian Sea

Status Very common in places

Similar species There are many closely related species, each occurring where the others do not—their ranges only rarely overlap

THE COMMON EUROPEAN TREEFROG lives in a variety of habitats, sometimes several hundred yards from water. It is most common in reed beds, however, or in bushes and shrubs around the edges of ponds. Juveniles tend to live lower down among the vegetation, and they often occur in large numbers in waist-high vegetation, while the adults—having climbed into higher parts of trees and shrubs—are nowhere to be seen. They hide during the day in hot, dry weather but may bask in an exposed position on days when the air is not too dry. When resting in an exposed position, they often turn bright yellowish green in color.

In Spain and Portugal while the treefrog's range overlaps that of the stripeless treefrog, *Hyla meridionalis*, it is often found at higher elevations (presumably because it tolerates lower temperatures), so the two species are not in direct competition. In the Canary Islands the stripeless treefrog tolerates very hot conditions and often occurs in banana plantations, where it breeds in irrigation ditches.

Raucous Choruses
Breeding takes place in shallow ponds that can be quite small. Water temperature is an important factor, and ponds in exposed positions are favored over those with overhanging trees or bushes. Males call from the water's surface when floating among aquatic vegetation. Their call is loud and raucous. If there are only two or three males calling, they usually synchronize, but once large numbers start up, the choruses soon become haphazard. They often continue

Captions to photographs provide additional information about each animal's lifestyle

Cross-references to relevant pages in this and other volumes

46 SEE ALSO Treefrogs 43:32; Treefrog, American Green 43:48

A number of other features help you navigate through the volumes and present you with helpful extra information. At the bottom of many pages are **cross-references** to other articles of interest. They may be to related animals, animals that live in similar places, or that have similar behavior, predators (or prey), lifestyles, and much more. Each volume also contains a **Set Index** to the complete *World of Animals: Amphibians and Reptiles*. Animals mentioned in the text are indexed by common and scientific names, and many topics are also covered. There is also a **Glossary** that will help you understand certain technical words. Each volume includes lists of useful **Further Reading and Websites** that help you take your research further.

Introductory article describes family or closely related groups

Graphic full-color photographs bring text to life

Easy-to-read and comprehensive text

Detailed diagrams illustrate text

Tables summarize classification of groups

Who's Who tables summarize classification of each major group

Introductory article describes major groups of animals

At-a-glance boxes cover topics of special interest

Meticulous drawings illustrate a typical selection of group members

Find the Animal

World of Animals: Amphibians and Reptiles is the fifth part of a library that describes all groups of living animals. Each cluster of volumes in *World of Animals* covers a familiar group of animals—mammals, birds, reptiles and amphibians, fish, and insects and other invertebrates.

The Animal Kingdom

The living world is divided into five kingdoms, one of which (kingdom Animalia) is the main subject of the *World of Animals*. Kingdom Animalia is divided into major groups called phyla. The phylum Chordata contains those animals that have a backbone—mammals, birds, reptiles, amphibians, and fish. Animals without backbones (so-called invertebrates, such as insects, spiders, mollusks, and crustaceans) belong to many different phyla. To find which set of volumes in the *World of Animals* you need, see the chart below.

World of Animals: Amphibians and Reptiles deals with two of the oldest lineages of land animals—the amphibians, which evolved from fish some 400 million years ago, and the reptiles, which evolved from amphibians about 350 million years ago. Although they are no longer dominant animals on earth (unlike the early reptiles typified by the dinosaurs), over 5,000 amphibian species and 8,000 species of reptiles can still be found. Most live in warmer or tropical regions of the world.

Naming Animals

To discuss animals, names are needed for the different kinds. Western diamondback rattlesnakes are one kind of snake, and sidewinders are another.

Rank	Scientific name	Common name
Kingdom	Animalia	Animals
Phylum	Chordata	Animals with a backbone
Class	Reptilia	Reptiles
Order	Squamata	Lizards, Snakes, Amphisbaenians
Suborder	Serpentes	Snakes
Family	Viperidae	Vipers and Pit Vipers
Genus	*Crotalus*	Rattlesnakes
Species	*Crotalus atrox*	Western diamondback rattlesnake

The kingdom Animalia is subdivided into phyla, classes, orders, families, genera, and species. Above is the classification for the western diamondback rattlesnake.

All western diamondback rattlesnakes look alike, breed together, and produce young like themselves. This distinction corresponds closely to the zoologists' definition of a species.

Zoologists use an internationally recognized system for naming species consisting of two-word scientific names, usually in Latin or Greek. The western diamondback rattlesnake is called *Crotalus atrox,* and the sidewinder *Crotalus cerastes. Crotalus* is the name of the genus (a group of very similar species); *atrox* or *cerastes* indicates the species in the genus. The same scientific names are recognized the world over. However, a species

⊕ *This chart lists the phyla in two of the five kingdoms. The phylum Arthropoda makes up a high proportion of all invertebrate animals.*

⊕ *The main groups of animals alive today. Volumes that cover each major group are indicated below.*

ANIMALS
Kingdom Animalia

SINGLE-CELLED LIFE
Kingdom Protista

Vertebrates/ Chordates
Phylum Chordata

Invertebrates
Numerous Phyla

Mammals
Class Mammalia
Volumes 1–10

Birds
Class Aves
Volumes 11–20

Reptiles
Class Reptilia
Volumes 44–50

Amphibians
Class Amphibia
Volumes 41–43

Fish
Several classes
Volumes 31–40

Insects, spiders, mollusks, spiny-skinned animals, worms
Volumes 21–30

Single-Celled Life
Volume 21 (part)

Groups of Amphibians and Reptiles

may have been described and named at different times without the zoologists realizing it was one species.

Classification allows us to make statements about larger groups of animals. For example, all rattlesnakes are vipers—along with other vipers they are placed in the family Viperidae. All vipers are placed with all other snakes in the suborder Serpentes; snakes are related to lizards, which are in the suborder Sauria, and so these two groups combine to form the order Squamata in the class Reptilia.

An important point must be made about the current scientific knowledge of these animals. New discoveries are being made every day, from the biology of individual creatures to the finding and naming of new species. Our knowledge of the relationships among the different groups is changing constantly. In addition, the number of species known increases all the time, particularly in the light of the very latest DNA analysis techniques that are available to zoologists.

TURTLES

The order Testudines encompasses all the reptiles variously known as turtles, terrapins, and tortoises. The order was formerly known as Chelonia; as a result, this group of reptiles is often referred to collectively as "chelonians." There is no strict rule about the use of the popular names, although the word "turtle" is frequently applied entirely for marine species. In North America there is a tendency to use this description for all aquatic forms, including those found in fresh water, although the term "terrapin" may be applied in some cases. Land forms are often described as tortoises and are identifiable by their relatively domed appearance.

The most obvious feature common to turtles as a group is the presence of a body casing in the form of a shell. It enables the reptile to withdraw its head, limbs, and tail to a variable extent, giving protection against predators. The shell itself is made up of two parts, and the individual segments of the shell are known as scutes.

The scutes can be colored to provide camouflage (known as crytic coloration). They are also distinctive enough so that, like fingerprints, they enable individuals to be identified. The scutes correspond to the epidermis, or outer layer of skin, in soft-skinned animals, and they lie on top of the bony layer. Just as in a brick wall, the links in the bony layer do not correspond exactly to the pattern of scutes directly above, which adds to the strength of the shell structure. The upper part of the shell is described as the carapace, and the underside is known as the plastron. The two areas are connected by so-called bridges that extend down each side of the body and are also made of the same material as the scutes.

The First Chelonians

The emergence of turtles as a group dates back to the late Carboniferous Period about 280 million years ago. The first examples are believed to have been rather like armadillos, with a semiflexible body casing that gave them some protection as well as allowing them reasonable freedom of movement. The first clearly recognizable forerunners of today's chelonians have been

→ *Turtles are at their most graceful in open water. This young loggerhead turtle,* Caretta caretta, *uses its powerful front limbs to "fly" through the ocean off the Azores.*

unearthed in rocks in Germany dating back to the Triassic Period approximately 220 million years ago. They were similar to the turtles of today, but unlike today's turtles, they had teeth both in their jaws and extending across the roof of the mouth. The distinctive pattern of scutes had already developed across the carapace. There were typically four, but occasionally five, vertebral scutes running down the center of the body, protecting the spinal column beneath. There were five corresponding scutes over the ribs (costal scutes) on each side of the vertebral scutes, and there were many smaller scutes around the edge of the shell, corresponding to the marginal scutes seen in chelonians today. These early

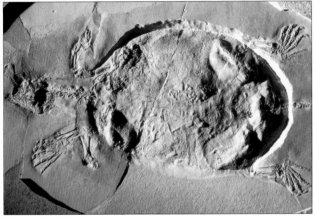

⬆ *Fossil turtles dating back to the Triassic Period have been found in limestone deposits in Germany. They share many characteristics with today's turtles, including the development of scutes on the carapace.*

forms were aquatic. Only much later in their evolutionary history did some turtles start to colonize land. They were apparently similar in size to freshwater turtles seen today, with a maximum shell length of about 24 inches (60 cm).

Turtles appear to have spread quite widely during the Jurassic Period (which began 200 million years ago) and continued their anatomical development. The teeth disappeared, and the shell began to fuse more completely. However, the early turtles were unable to take full advantage of its protection, because they could not withdraw their head or their limbs under the bony casing. It is believed that turtles increased significantly in size

during the Cretaceous Period, which ended about 65 million years ago with the demise of the dinosaurs. The increase in size may have been triggered partly in response to the massive predators that had developed in the seas of that era. The largest member of the order ever recorded, known as *Archelon*, had a shell that measured at least 12 feet (3.7 m) long. This is a third longer than that of the leatherback, *Dermochelys coriacea*, which is the biggest turtle in the world's oceans today.

Retracting the Neck

As turtles evolved, two separate mechanisms for retracting the neck into the front opening between the carapace and the plastron developed. Today turtles are described as belonging to one or the other of two groups: the side-necked turtles (suborder Pleurodira), which retract their necks horizontally, or the hidden-necked turtles (suborder Cryptodira), which retract their necks vertically.

All turtles have eight cervical (neck) vertebrae, but those of members of the suborder Pleurodira are more developed. The dorsal spines running down the top of the neck bones are taller, and the transverse processes on the sides of the vertebrae are also enlarged, allowing for the attachment of muscles that retract the head to the side, leaving the neck and head a little exposed at the front of the shell. This group includes the snake-necked turtles, some of which have necks that are longer than the shell.

The vertebrae of members of the other group (the suborder Cryptodira) are reduced, making the neck more flexible and allowing the turtle to withdraw it into the shell by folding it back on itself in a tight vertical "s" shape. Most of them can withdraw their head completely inside the shell. All but two of today's families of chelonians belong to this latter group, including all those in North America, Europe, and mainland Asia.

Specialized Body Parts

The skeletal structure of turtles has become highly specialized. The cervical vertebrae are flexible. The next section of the vertebral column, extending right down to the tail, is fused within the carapace. But the tail itself is very mobile. Since the ribs are fused within the shell, they cannot be used for respiratory purposes. Instead, turtles rely on respiratory muscles located around the leg pockets. They force air out of the lungs, which are themselves quite rigid structures. Breathing in occurs as a result of the lower pressure in the turtle's body. In the case of aquatic chelonians the surrounding water creates extra pressure on the turtle's body. As a result, breathing in requires more muscular activity than breathing out.

Aquatic chelonians breathe when they surface; but some, such as the softshells in the family Trionychidae, are also able to extract oxygen from water in their cloaca, so they do not need to surface as regularly. These particular turtles, along with the matamata, *Chelus fimbriatus*, also have elongated nostrils that act like snorkels, allowing them to breathe without having to break the water surface. Some species in the Trionychidae, for example, *Trionyx*, can also extract oxygen directly from water in the pharyngeal region at the back of the throat. This area is highly vascularized (supplied with blood vessels) for this purpose, and water is exhaled through the nostrils.

Turtles' limbs are protected by a covering of scales, and their feet end in claws. In the case of tortoises the

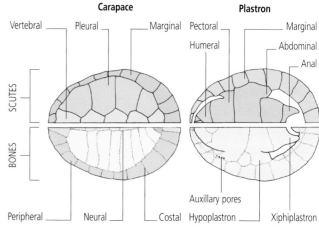

↑ *Carapace structure. Side-necked turtles (suborder Pleurodira) have 13 scutes and 9–11 bones in the plastron, and the pelvis is fused to the shell. Hidden-necked turtles (suborder Cryptodira) have 11–12 plastral scutes and 8–9 plastral bones.*

claws tend to be relatively broad and blunt, since they wear them down as they walk. In aquatic chelonians they are often much narrower and sharper. This is partly because some of them use their claws to tear food apart while holding it in their jaws before swallowing it. In the case of the sliders, *Pseudemys* species (family Emydidae), the claws are a means of distinguishing the sexes, since the front claws are much longer in males. They use these claws as part of their courtship ritual to fan water gently in the face of a female and touch her chin.

Many turtles, for example, the loggerhead musk turtle, *Sternotherus minor*, have small fleshy swellings known as barbels in the chin area. They are well supplied with nerves and play an important part in scent detection. They also have a tactile function, providing information to the turtle as it moves over the substrate. This is especially valuable in turbid waters, where visibility is poor.

The Senses

All chelonians rely on their sense of smell to figure out what is edible and to find a mate. This function is linked with Jacobson's organ, a structure in the roof of the mouth connected to the brain. Turtles can detect scents under water. They can also see well and have color vision, which

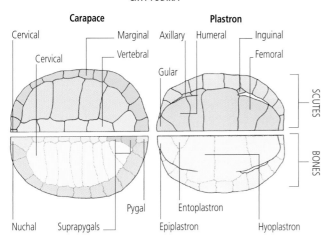

CRYPTODIRA

Carapace

Cervical · Marginal
Cervical · Vertebral

Nuchal · Suprapygals · Pygal

Plastron

Axillary · Humeral · Inguinal
Gular · Femoral

SCUTES

BONES

Epiplastron · Entoplastron · Hyoplastron

may help tortoises in particular locate fruits and plants some distance away. Hearing is not a significant sense in turtles generally. They have no external ear openings, but the tympanic membrane is evident on each side of the head behind the eyes. This may explain why they rarely vocalize except when mating.

All turtles reproduce by means of eggs, but clutch size varies dramatically according to species, ranging from a single egg to relatively large clutches numbering over 100 in some cases.

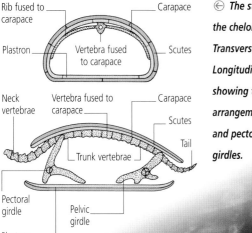

Rib fused to carapace · Carapace
Plastron · Vertebra fused to carapace · Scutes

Neck vertebrae · Vertebra fused to carapace · Carapace
Scutes
Trunk vertebrae · Tail
Pectoral girdle · Pelvic girdle
Plastron

⊖ *The structure of the chelonian shell. Transverse section (1). Longitudinal section (2), showing the arrangement of pelvic and pectoral girdles.*

⊕ *The eastern box turtle,* Terrapene carolina *from the southeastern United States, is one of the chelonians that have colonized land. It can be found in forests or meadows wherever there is enough moisture.*

Marine Turtles

There are seven surviving species of marine turtles occurring in the world's oceans today. Although they tend to be encountered most often in tropical waters, it is not uncommon for some species to range much more widely, well into temperate latitudes. In the Atlantic they can occasionally be seen off the northern coast of Scandinavia. These chelonians are strictly aquatic. Males spend their entire lives at sea, while females only haul themselves out through the surf for a brief period overnight to lay their eggs before returning immediately to the ocean.

On land their large flippers are cumbersome, lying almost at right angles to the body, but in the sea they enable these large reptiles to swim elegantly and with minimum effort. They can also move surprisingly fast in water, achieving speeds approaching 20 miles per hour (32 kph). Sea turtles have webbing between the toes of all four limbs, linking the toes together (as in many waterbirds) and giving more propulsion through the water. However, the hind legs do not play an important role in locomotion. Instead, they act like a rudder to help them steer.

Turtles under Threat

One of the major problems faced by sea turtles is the danger of being hunted by humans in the tropical areas where they nest. They are very vulnerable once they emerge from their natural habitat. In some areas numbers of these turtles on their traditional nesting beaches have fallen dramatically. Kemp's ridley, *Lepidochelys kempi*, is especially under threat, since its main nesting grounds are on a single stretch of beach in Mexico that is about 12 miles (19 km) in length. (Other marine turtles have much more widespread breeding grounds.) Local people used to describe the mass appearance of the Kemp's ridley females as the *arribadas*, or "arrival." The turtles waited offshore in the shallows until conditions were favorable and then came ashore as a group.

When this remarkable event was first filmed for a television documentary in 1947, there were approximately 40,000 turtles, but the number visiting the beach annually shrank to just 5,000 within 20 years. This shows a very rapid population decline; and since young turtles take at least 20 years to reach sexual maturity, the downturn in numbers has proved to be long-lasting as well.

Turtles are solitary by nature, so it is very hard to gain any insight into the size of their population once they leave their nesting grounds. But it is not only predation on nesting beaches that can be harmful to their numbers. Events offshore can be equally catastrophic. Kemp's ridley, for example, is not primarily vegetarian in its feeding habits but hunts crustaceans such as shrimp. Up to 500 of these turtles were being killed annually in shrimp nets, which was undoubtedly having a marked effect on their numbers until steps were taken to reduce the losses.

Scientists have tried various means of safeguarding the future of threatened populations of sea turtles, including attempts to protect their nesting grounds. Unfortunately, in the Mediterranean region, for example, turtles lay their eggs on some of the most desirable

---

Common name Marine turtles **Order** Testudines

Family Cheloniidae—6 species in 4 genera, the loggerhead turtle, *Caretta caretta*; green turtle, *C. mydas*; flatback turtle, *Natator depressus*; hawksbill turtle, *Eretmochelys imbricata*; Kemp's ridley, *Lepidochelys kempi*; olive ridley, *L. olivacea*

Family Dermochelyidae—1 species in 1 genus, the leatherback turtle, *Dermochelys coriacea*

 SEE ALSO Turtles **47**:8; Turtle, Loggerhead **47**:16; Turtle, Green **47**:18; Turtle, Leatherback **47**:24

↑ *A female olive ridley turtle,* Lepidochelys olivacea, *waits until dusk to make her way onto a beach in Costa Rica to lay her eggs. She will probably return to the same nesting place each year that she breeds.*

← *Turtle eggs are vulnerable to predation. This recently hatched clutch of olive ridley turtles,* Lepidochelys olivacea, *is under attack from a stork and a group of black vultures on a nesting beach in Costa Rica.*

beaches, and waterfront development in these places has meant that turtles have suffered. Although strong lighting does not seem to deter most females from nesting, when the young hatch, they often mistakenly move toward the strong light in the opposite direction from the sea.

Sea turtles are very loyal to their own hatching grounds, which means that moving breeding populations is difficult. However, helping the young through the critical early stages—for example, by removing eggs from nests and hatching them in captivity before returning them to the sea—can result in far higher numbers making the journey out to sea. There are a host of natural predators that are likely to congregate on turtle nesting beaches, ranging from lizards to birds, that will either dig up the eggs or seize the hatchlings as they try to scramble to the sea after having dug their way out of the sand. It is no coincidence that huge numbers of hatchling turtles emerge at the same time under cover of darkness. By emerging en masse, a relatively higher proportion of them are likely to make it into the surf. Once they are in the water, however, predatory seabirds may still swoop down and seize the young turtles.

According to studies carried out with turtles hatched artificially and released off the coast of Borneo, as many as six in every 10 young turtles that make it this far will be taken by predators within the first two hours of entering the sea. The young swim at speeds of up to 1 mile per hour (1.6 kph). At first the waves are the main navigational force, but it appears that the earth's magnetic field gradually becomes more significant to the turtles as a means of orientation.

Seaweed Sanctuaries

There are certain areas in the oceans where young turtles are known to congregate, usually associated with the drifting mats of seaweed known as sargassum. These mats not only provide the turtles with camouflage close to the surface, they also provide a plentiful supply of food—plankton, small jellyfish, crustaceans, and fish are all found in this marine environment. The young turtles generally appear to remain in this type of habitat for years before eventually returning to near their nesting grounds.

In breeding years female turtles return to their nesting beaches several times to lay eggs, but most species do not breed every year. Kemp's ridley is an exception, breeding every year, which may give the species a better chance of surviving. In other species it can be five years or more before the female returns to breed again. Male turtles may also migrate back to these areas, mating offshore with females. But they may also mate randomly in the oceans. It is thought that female sea turtles, in common with other chelonians, do not need to mate just before egg laying, since they are capable of storing sperm in their reproductive tract. This enables them to lay fertile eggs for two years or more after mating.

⊕ *A group of flatback turtle hatchlings,* Natator depressus, *on a beach in Queensland, Australia. Up to 60 eggs are laid in a clutch, but the chance of more than half the hatchlings surviving to adulthood is small.*

Tracking Sea Turtles

Scientists have used various methods to chart the movements of sea turtles once they leave their nesting beaches. Flipper tags have proved a relatively reliable and cheap method of study for a long time, with their codes revealing where the individual in question came from. The problem is that this method depends on recovering the turtle and gives no indication of where it may have been during the months or years since it was last recorded.

A more informative but much more expensive system of tracking involves the use of satellite transmitters. They need to be firmly attached to the turtle's carapace, and unfortunately, the antennae of these units are vulnerable to being damaged on rocks or even during mating. Such devices can provide a wealth of information, however, including details about the turtle's swimming speed, how far it dives, and its movements in comparison with prevailing ocean currents.

This tracking system is already providing data that are proving valuable in contributing to a better understanding of the habits of these reptiles. It has become clear, for example, that one of the main reasons why Kemp's ridleys, *Lepidochelys kempi*, become caught in shrimp nets off the coast of Mexico is because they do not swim through the deeper water in the Gulf of Mexico. Instead, they prefer to move along the coast, swimming in water less than 150 feet (46 m) deep.

Other scientific advances are being used in combination with satellite tracking to provide a better insight into the reproductive behavior of turtles. Samples taken from nesting turtles help build up genetic profiles of populations on the basis of their DNA. This information can be combined with tracking studies to show where the turtles part company. This has already turned up some interesting results. Not all populations travel great distances. For example, hawksbill turtles, *Eretmochelys imbricata*, nesting on the Seychelles tend to stay close to those particular islands throughout their lives.

A loggerhead turtle, Caretta caretta, is measured before being tagged and released into the sea off the coast of Florida.

Common name Loggerhead turtle

Scientific name *Caretta caretta*

Family Cheloniidae

Suborder Cryptodira

Order Testudines

Size Carapace 41 in (104 cm) long

Weight Up to 1,200 lb (544 kg)

Key features Very big head and powerful jaws; carapace heart shaped, lacking ridges in adults (but juvenile's carapace is ridged); carapace brown, often with light brown, reddish-brown, or black markings; plastron yellowish-brown in color; limbs paddlelike and have 2 claws on each

Habits Tends to breed farther from the equator than many turtles; relatively aggressive

Breeding Nesting interval typically 2–3 years but can range from 1–6 years; females come ashore to lay clutches of 100 eggs 4–7 times during the breeding season; eggs hatch after 54–68 days

Diet Mainly shellfish, including mussels, clams, and crabs; may eat some seaweed

Habitat Coastal areas, often in relatively shallow water; occurs in muddy waters as well as clear tropical seas

Distribution Wide range through the Pacific, Indian, and Atlantic Oceans, especially in southeastern United States; occurs as far north as Newfoundland and as far south as Argentina

Status Endangered (IUCN); listed on CITES Appendix I

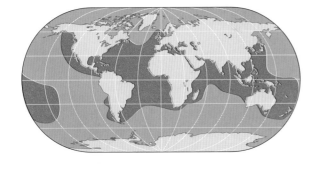

Loggerhead Turtle

Caretta caretta

The loggerhead turtle is one of the largest of the hard-shelled turtles. Despite a ban on international trade, the turtle is still considered to be vulnerable worldwide.

THE LOGGERHEAD IS THE LARGEST MEMBER of its family. Its skull length alone can be almost 12 inches (30 cm) and gives the turtle its common name. Its powerful jaws are used to crush the shells of invertebrates such as horseshoe crabs that feature prominently in its diet. The southeastern United States is one of its strongholds, with the beaches here being used by over one-third of the world's population. It is the commonest species seen by divers off the coast of Florida, where it frequents relatively shallow waters.

Nesting typically occurs between late August and the end of September in Florida, which is the most significant nesting area in the region. Small numbers of female loggerheads also lay their eggs on beaches in the Carolinas and Georgia. In both places they dig holes in which to lay their eggs, and the eggs take on average 54 days to hatch in Florida, extending to between 63 and 68 days in Georgia.

Cutting the Egg

When it is ready to hatch, the young turtle uses the sharp projection on the end of its nose, the egg tooth, to cut its way out. The plastron is curved when it hatches and straightens out later. Having nourished the young turtle during its development in the egg and for a while immediately after hatching, the yolk sac is soon absorbed into the body.

It usually takes about five days from the time that young loggerheads start breaking out of their shells until they appear at the surface of the sand. They often rest during this period, especially during the day when the sand above them is hotter. This instinctive reaction ensures that they only emerge under cover of darkness, when it is safer. The young loggerhead hatchlings measure just 2 inches (5 cm) and vary in color from light to dark brown on the carapace with yellowish underparts. The flippers are brown with very distinctive white edges.

Drawn to the Light

As in other sea turtles, young loggerheads orient themselves by light at first. They are instinctively drawn to the sea, where the light above is usually brighter than on land. Unfortunately, in areas where there has been marked beachfront development, the light from the

The Threat of Nets

Because they live mainly in relatively shallow coastal waters where they look for rich shellfish beds, loggerhead turtles are vulnerable to becoming entangled in shrimp nets and drowning as a result. Although they generally do not catch fish, they sometimes scavenge on dead fish used as bait; this habit can also lead to the turtles becoming caught in traps.

⊙ The head of the loggerhead turtle is relatively large compared with that of other turtles. In open sea loggerheads spend much of the time floating on the surface and feed on sponges, jellyfish, mussels, clams, oysters, shrimp, as well as a variety of fish.

land confuses young turtles and pulls them away from the sea. Weakened and disoriented, they are vulnerable to predators on the beach when dawn breaks.

Hatchling loggerheads that reach the water swim during the day and rest at night as they head to areas of sargassum in the ocean. It is thought that they drift in the fields of sargassum, traveling as far the Azores, which lie some 2,500 miles (4,023 km) from the beaches of Florida where they hatched. They remain there until they attain a shell length of about 20 in (50 cm) and probably return to the area around Florida for the first time 10 years later. Loggerheads are as likely to be found in muddy waters with poor visibility as they are to occur in clear tropical seas.

The turtles range along a vast area of the Atlantic coast and have been seen as far north as Newfoundland and as far south as Argentina. Juveniles in particular are found in large numbers well away from their traditional haunts. As many as 10,000 loggerheads are estimated to spend the summer months off the Chesapeake Bay region of the eastern United States, appearing from May onward. They overwinter in warmer waters farther south.

Young turtles that hatch in the Indian and Pacific Oceans are thought to head for the coast of Baja California. Huge numbers of juvenile loggerheads have been found there, and their movements have been confirmed by satellite tracking.

Common name Green turtle

Scientific name
 Chelonia mydas

Family Cheloniidae

Suborder Cryptodira

Order Testudines

Size Carapace usually over 36 in (91 cm) long

Weight Up to 352 lb (160 kg) when adult

Key features Head relatively small with a prominent pair of scales in front of the eyes; jaw is serrated along its edges; distinctive differences in appearance between Atlantic and Pacific populations, the latter having a significantly darker plastron; carapace dome shaped and appears green; limbs paddlelike, usually with a single claw on each one

Habits A marine turtle occurring in coastal areas rather than roaming across the open ocean; some populations bask during the day

Breeding Female lays about 115 eggs per clutch on average 3–5 times during a season; interval between laying is usually 2–3 years; eggs hatch after about 65 days

Diet Small individuals feed on small crustaceans and similar creatures; larger individuals are entirely herbivorous, eating sea grass and marine algae

Habitat Coastal areas, bays, and shallow water in tropical and temperate seas

Distribution Pacific and Atlantic Oceans

Status Endangered (IUCN); listed on CITES Appendix I

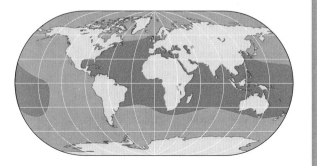

Green Turtle

Chelonia mydas

The green turtle was once common in the warm oceans of the world. Unfortunately, it has become increasingly rare in some areas, where it suffers from commercial exploitation and is at risk of extinction.

THE NAME GREEN TURTLE COMES FROM the color of the fat beneath the shell in these marine turtles. It varies among individuals: In some there may be light stripes radiating across the carapace with yellow and brown areas apparent as well. The Pacific population is often described as black sea turtles because they typically have a much darker, grayish, or even black carapace. Their shells also appear more domed than those of their Atlantic relatives.

Green turtles are probably the slowest growing of all vertebrates thanks largely to their diet. Although initially they hunt small crustaceans, they soon become vegetarian, feeding mainly on sea grass and marine algae once their carapace measures approximately 8 inches (20 cm) long. In areas where sea grass is prevalent, regular grazing by the turtles encourages the plant's growth. This is important to the turtles' own well-being, since fresh shoots are more nutritious. As in herbivorous mammals, the green turtles rely on a beneficial population of microbes in their intestinal tract to aid the digestion of plant matter.

Dietary Adaptations

Green turtles are quite adaptable in their feeding habits, and their diet varies significantly throughout their range. In northern Australia, for example, they have learned to snap the leaves off mangrove trees, adding to their feeding options. The serrations on the sides of their jaws help them tear off mouthfuls that can be swallowed easily, and they will sometimes even pluck leaves growing above the water's surface.

In areas where sea grass is not present, notably around Hawaii and on Australia's Great

⬆ *A green turtle feeds on marine algae growing on coral in waters off the coast of Malaysia. Its other favorite food is sea grass.*

⬅ *The beautiful markings of the carapace can be seen clearly on this green turtle from Malaysia. The green effect comes from the layer of fat beneath the shell.*

Barrier Reef, the lack of sea grass may explain why green turtles there are so slow to reach sexual maturity. Studies involving Hawaiian green turtles revealed that some were mature by 11 years old, but others were not capable of breeding for the first time until they were 59. In the case of some green turtles living off the coast of Queensland, Australia, sexual maturity may not occur until the turtles are 70 years old. Growth and therefore breeding capability relate largely to the availability of food. Ultimately,

Temperature-Dependent Sex Determination

It was in green turtles that researchers first discovered the phenomenon of temperature-dependent sex determination (TDSD). It is now known to apply quite widely to many chelonians that lack sex chromosomes to regulate gender. In such cases the temperature at which the eggs are incubated is significant in determining the sex of the hatchlings. Clutches exposed to higher temperatures contain female offspring, while those that hatch under cooler conditions are likely to produce mainly males. However, the exact details vary according to species, and TDSD does not apply to all species.

however, the green turtle can grow larger than any other member of its family. Those in the Atlantic are bigger on average than their Pacific counterparts.

Sand Pits

When they come ashore to nest, females dig a pit for their eggs, using their hind flippers. This laborious task usually takes about two hours. A nesting female must do this roughly every two weeks during the breeding season, since she lays from two to seven clutches. As in other marine turtles, the eggs have relatively rubbery shells and are laid with mucus around them. This stops them from being damaged as they fall on top of each other in the pit. The female uses her flippers to cover the eggs with sand.

Because the eggs are laid above the high-tide line, they are free from the risk of flooding and should hatch about 65 days later. Hatchling green turtles

Basking

A very unusual behavior pattern has been observed in green turtles found in the northwestern area of the Hawaiian archipelago. Individuals haul themselves out of the water onto the beaches of isolated islands to bask during the day. Why they do this is unclear, but it may be a way of avoiding attacks from tiger sharks, *Galeocerdo cuvier*, which are prevalent in the area. Basking is almost completely unknown in other marine turtles.

Once established in an area, the turtles are unlikely to leave except to nest. They also seem to be particular about their feeding preferences. In Hawaiian waters green turtles regularly look for just nine out of over 400 species of marine algae growing in the region.

⊕ *Using her hind flippers and becoming covered in sand in the process, a nesting female green turtle digs a pit for her eggs on a beach on Ascension Island.*

are about 2 inches (5 cm) long and weigh roughly 0.9 ounces (25g). Their carapace is dark above and lighter below. Young green turtles that hatch on Hawaiian beaches face relatively few predators. Seabirds do not seriously affect their numbers, nor do large fish waiting offshore in the ocean.

Populations around the World

Green turtles are widely distributed throughout temperate and tropical seas, and have been seen off the North American coast as far north as Massachusetts.

In the past green turtles were heavily hunted as a source of food, but in many parts of their range they are now strictly protected. Nicaragua shut its turtle-processing plants in 1976, a move that has probably also helped the important Tortuguero population in neighboring Costa Rica—today turtles of all ages can be seen feeding together there.

Although it is nearly 30 years since green turtles were given legal protection in Hawaii, their numbers have not increased dramatically. This is partly because of changes in their habitat that have reduced the amount of food available. In addition, a significant number are affected by skin tumors known as fibropapillomas, which may be linked with harmful environmental conditions. In the vicinity of the island of Honokowai over 90 percent of the green turtles are suffering with these viral growths on their bodies.

The green turtle population in the Atlantic has fallen dramatically in some areas, and the species has become extinct on the Cayman Islands and Bermuda. Breeding populations occur on the mainland right around the Caribbean from the coast of Florida to Costa Rica and down to Surinam in South America as well as on islands throughout the region.

Success Story

One of the most significant breeding colonies can be found on Ascension Island. The turtles nesting there have been tracked back to the coast of Brazil, which means that they must migrate over 1,600 miles (1,000 km) to their nesting grounds. Individuals within the Ascension Island breeding population represent some of the largest living examples of the species, possibly because they have not been subjected to heavy predation.

Even so, they would have been dwarfed by some of the monsters recorded from

centuries ago. Particularly large specimens weighing as much as 1,000 pounds (454 kg) have been recorded from the Cedar Key region of Florida.

Ranching

One of the practical ways of safeguarding wild populations of green turtles is by ranching. This entails collecting a percentage of the eggs laid by the turtles and hatching them artificially. The young hatchlings are reared in captivity and ultimately used to meet the demand for soup and other by-products.

By legitimizing trade in this way, it is hoped that wild turtles will be left alone. However, a number of welfare issues have arisen surrounding programs of this type, especially with regard to the turtles' growth rates. Young green turtles raised in this way grow at a much faster rate than in the wild. This affects their physical appearance, causing the carapace to appear more domed.

Fears have also been expressed that these programs simply encourage trade and could provide cover for the illegal collection of wild turtles, which are killed and sold as if they were reared in captivity. International trade in marine turtles (and various associated products ranging from soup to shells that may be sold to unsuspecting tourists) remains illegal under the Conservation in International Trade in Endangered Species (CITES) treaty.

⊕ It is hoped that turtle farms such as this one on Grand Cayman Island will prevent the hunting of green turtles in the wild.

Common name
Hawksbill turtle

Scientific name *Eretmochelys imbricata*

Family Cheloniidae

Suborder Cryptodira

Order Testudines

Size Carapace up to 36 in (91 cm) long

Weight Up to 150 lb (68 kg)

Key features Head narrow and distinctive with a hawklike bill; 2 pairs of scales in front of the eyes; carapace elliptical with an attractive blend of yellow or orange mixed with brown, but coloration is highly individual; scutes overlap behind each other on the carapace; 2 claws present on each flipper; serrations present on side of carapace

Habits Often encountered looking for prey on coral reefs

Breeding Female usually lays up to 160 eggs in a season but breeds on average only every 2–4 years; eggs hatch after 58–75 days

Diet Invertebrates, mainly sponges, but also squid and shrimp

Habitat Mainly tropical waters

Distribution Occurs in the Atlantic and in parts of the Indian and Pacific oceans

Status Endangered (IUCN); listed on CITES Appendix I

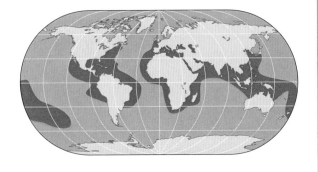

Hawksbill Turtle

Eretmochelys imbricata

The name imbricata *describes the overlapping plates on the hawksbill's upper shell. Unfortunately, it is the beautiful carapace, known as "tortoiseshell," that has led to widespread hunting of this small sea turtle.*

RECENT SURVEYS SUGGEST THAT numbers of the hawksbill turtle have declined more seriously and rapidly in recent years than was previously thought. This is true especially throughout the Caribbean and the western Atlantic Ocean in spite of the widespread protection given to the species. In the past huge numbers of these turtles were caught. Their shells were used to create "tortoiseshell" objects ranging from tea caddies to hair combs, which were highly fashionable in the late 19th and early 20th centuries. The scutes that extend over the carapace are the most highly prized because of the amber mottling that is apparent once the upper shell of the turtle is polished. In Japan, where the use of tortoiseshell has been elevated to an art form, this material is known as *bekko*.

Deadly Sponges

The hawksbill turtles get their name from the shape of their narrow mouthparts. Their "v"-shaped lower jaw is used to reach and pluck sponges from inaccessible areas of a reef. Some species of sponge protect themselves by toxins in their bodies, but they do not seem to harm the hawksbill turtle. Bizarrely, the sponge toxins remain potent, a fact confirmed by cases in which humans died from eating the flesh of hawksbill turtles that had eaten the sponges.

The turtles depend on sponges as their major food source. Any deterioration in the conditions on a reef will cause a decline in the number of sponges and leave the turtles vulnerable to starvation.

Hawksbill turtles are relatively small and agile, and can therefore reach nesting beaches

Hitching a Ride

Sea turtles in general carry a number of other creatures on their shell, particularly barnacles and various types of coral. Hawksbills from the Atlantic region often have Columbus crabs, *Planes minutus*, attached to the rear of their body. They are probably acquired when the hatchling turtles are feeding in the sargassum, where young crabs are frequently found.

In contrast, it is normally adult crabs that are seen on mature turtles. They help keep the reptile's body clean, feeding on algae and other creatures that may also attach themselves. If the crabs did not keep these organisms in check, they could make swimming much harder for the reptile by reducing its streamlined profile.

over reefs that would exclude larger, heavier species. They lay their eggs quite high up on the beach, often in sites partially concealed by vegetation. Once on land, the nesting process can be completed in an hour, although it often takes longer. Females lay a total of up to 160 eggs, returning to the same beach to lay at intervals of roughly 14 days about four or five times during the season. The number of eggs laid is determined by the size of the female, with larger turtles laying more eggs.

Dangerous Detritus

The hatchlings have a carapace length of just over 1.5 in (3.8 cm), and they generally weigh less than 0.7 ounces (20 g). They head into areas of sargassum at first and are vulnerable to floating detritus, including pieces of styrofoam, which can sometimes lodge in their digestive tracts with fatal consequences. Assuming they survive, the young turtles head back to reef areas once they have grown to 8 inches (20 cm) long—they often retreat under rocky overhangs and similar safe places.

The carapace alters in shape as young hawksbills mature, taking on a more elongated outline. The serrations running down the sides toward the rear of the carapace may have a protective function, but they shrink as the turtle grows older. Their ultimate disappearance in adults is regarded as a sign of old age.

Many hawksbill turtles do not seem to travel long distances to their nesting grounds, but there are exceptions, discovered as a result of tagging. One female caught and marked in the Torres Strait region of northern Australia was caught again 11 months later approximately 2,240 miles (3,600 km) away in the Solomon Islands, where she came on land to nest.

⊖ *A hawksbill turtle swims near the Virgin Islands in the Caribbean. The closeup shows the beaklike mouthparts that give the turtle its common name.*

23

Leatherback Turtle

Dermochelys coriacea

Common name Leatherback turtle

Scientific name *Dermochelys coriacea*

Family Dermochelyidae

Suborder Cryptodira

Order Testudines

Size Carapace can be up to 8 ft (2.4 m) in length

Weight Up to 1,650 lb (750 kg)

Key features Carapace very distinctive with 7 ridges running down its length; surface of the carapace is effectively a rubbery skin rather than made up of scales; skin strengthened with very small bony plates; color dark with whitish markings; plastron bears about 5 ridges and varies in color from a whitish shade to black; flippers lack claws; front flippers extremely long; carapace of hatchlings has rows of white scales

Habits Often favors open sea, swimming widely through the world's oceans

Breeding Clutches consist of about 80 viable eggs; female typically produces 6–9 clutches per season; egg-laying interval typically 2–3 years; youngsters emerge after about 65 days

Diet Almost exclusively jellyfish

Habitat Temperate and tropical waters

Distribution Has the largest range of any marine turtle; found in all the world's oceans from Alaska to New Zealand

Status Critically Endangered (IUCN); listed on CITES Appendix I

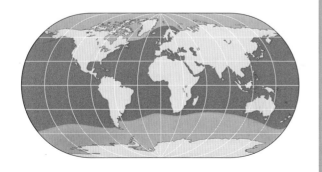

The leatherback turtles are true giants. They are the largest of all marine turtles and the heaviest reptiles in the world. Their very distinctive shells have a leathery appearance.

AT ABOUT 8 FEET (2.4 M) LONG and weighing up to 1,650 pounds (750 kg), the leatherback's bulk probably enables it to maintain a sufficiently high core body temperature that allows it to venture farther into temperate waters than any other species of marine turtle. Leatherbacks are apparently unaffected by sea temperatures even below 41°F (5°C), and they range as far north as the seas around Alaska. Their body is actually slightly warmer than that of their surroundings in these cold waters, which suggests that they have a basic mechanism to regulate their body temperature.

These turtles are also found in the oceans below the southern tip of Africa and off the Chilean coast as well as close to New Zealand. In fact, the largest leatherback recorded was not found in the tropics but was discovered stranded on a beach on the coast of Wales in the British Isles in 1988. It is possible that global warming and its effects on sea temperature are affecting the range of these turtles.

Remote Nesting Sites

Leatherbacks return to the tropics to breed. They often choose remote areas for this purpose, although there are about 50 nests recorded along the Florida coastline each year. They traditionally use beaches onto which they can haul themselves up without difficulty, and where they can come directly out of deep sea rather than swimming across reefs. This is possibly to protect their vulnerable underparts from injury and may explain why they tend to nest more commonly on mainland areas rather than islands. Unfortunately, these beaches can be badly eroded in storms, leaving the leatherback's developing eggs at greater risk of being lost than those of other marine turtles.

Egg stealing has been a threat in some areas in the past, but improved protective measures mean that it is less of a problem today. The oil in the leatherback's body was also used for the manufacture of many products, including cosmetics and medicines, but the introduction of synthetic substitutes has ended this trade. Leatherbacks are not hunted for their meat, which is regarded as unpalatable.

Although leatherbacks often lay eggs on their own, they sometimes nest in small groups. Their breeding range extends almost all the way around the world—from the Caribbean region across to the western coast of South Africa to India, Sri Lanka, Thailand, and Australia right across the Pacific to the shores of

Long Journeys

Tagging studies have revealed the remarkable distances that leatherbacks can cover in the world's oceans—one individual tagged on its nesting ground in Surinam, northern South America, was rediscovered on the eastern side of the Atlantic over 4,226 miles (6,800 km) from the original tagging site. Unfortunately, leatherbacks have tended to lose their tags more readily than other turtles, so fewer data are available, but it certainly appears that those encountered along the northern coast of South America regularly undertake journeys of over 3,125 miles (5,028 km). Switching the tag site on the leatherback's body from the front flipper to the inner side of the back flipper has helped, however, since the tags are exposed to less physical force in this area of the body. This should ensure that more information about their movements can be obtained.

Mexico. Clutch sizes laid by leatherbacks in the eastern Pacific region tend to be smaller than those produced in other parts of their range. What is suspected to be the largest breeding colony of leatherbacks in the world was only discovered as

⊍ *Female leatherbacks, such as this one in Trinidad, come ashore to nest every two to three years on the warm sands of remote tropical beaches.*

recently as 1976 thanks to the confiscation of a large number of leatherback eggs that were on their way to Mexico City. The trail led to an area known as Tierra Colorado on the Pacific coast.

Studies have since revealed that up to 500 leatherback females may come ashore to lay eggs there every night during the nesting period, mainly in December and January each year. It appears that, at least in this area, female

Death at the Hands of Humans

The leatherback's wide range means that it is very difficult to build up an accurate population estimate, but there are signs that the species is in trouble. This is not essentially because of hunting pressure but largely as a result of its feeding habits. Its rather slender jaws with their scissorlike action are used to capture jellyfish, which form the basis of its diet. Unfortunately, these turtles find it hard to distinguish between jellyfish and plastic detritus such as plastic bags and other similar waste floating on the surface of the sea. When seized and swallowed, these items are likely to get stuck in the turtle's gut, resulting in a slow and painful death. Controlling losses of leatherback turtles is exceptionally difficult, and there is no easy way of solving this problem.

There has been progress, however, in addressing some of the other threats facing leatherback populations. It was estimated that about 640 of these turtles were being accidentally captured in nets in U.S. waters annually. Many of them died through drowning or injuries sustained during their capture. Devices to keep turtles out of the nets were developed, and the law was changed to make their use mandatory in U.S. waters. Elsewhere, however (often in international waters), problems remain, with the turtles being caught in fishing nets or becoming entangled in ropes or lines. Even if the leatherback can free itself, the resulting injury can prove fatal. The leatherback's urge to swim, together with its specialized feeding habits, mean that nursing it back to health in captivity is often a difficult task too.

leatherbacks return on their own with no males congregating offshore in search of mates.

An unusual phenomenon is the presence of small, apparently immature eggs found in the nests of leatherback turtles. Their presence may be linked in some way to the interval of time between the laying of the clutches, which is much shorter than in other marine species. It is often no more than seven to 10 days, and some eggs do not develop fully in this time. It takes about 65 days for the young leatherbacks to hatch and emerge at the surface, by which stage they are about 2.5 inches (6.3 cm) long. The hatchlings are unmistakable: The longitudinal ridges are well defined, and there are rows of white scales that appear as stripes along the length of the flippers.

It is quite straightforward to determine the sex of leatherback turtles, since males have much longer tails than females and, as in many other chelonians, a slightly concave plastron.

Imprinting Behavior

One strange phenomenon that has been repeatedly documented is the way in which, after she has completed the task of egg laying, a female leatherback circles the nest site, just as the young do once they hatch. It may be that this behavior somehow imprints onto the memories of the youngsters, aiding their return to the same place in due course. Current estimates suggest that there could be between 100,000 and 115,000 breeding female leatherbacks in the world's oceans today.

Predators

Leatherbacks tend to dive deeper than other turtles, which may give them some protection against being attacked. They are also well equipped to swim fast out of harm's way thanks to the propulsive power of their front flippers. They are longer than those of any other marine turtle and can extend to nearly 9 feet (2.7 m) in length.

Even once they are fully grown, however, these turtles still face a number of predators. Various sharks, including the notorious great

⊕ *A leatherback turtle hatching on the Virgin Islands in the Caribbean. Hatchlings use a sharp tooth called an "egg tooth" to break through the eggshell.*

⊕ *In French Guiana a group of young hatchlings have just emerged from their eggs. They must make their way to the ocean quickly to avoid predatory seabirds.*

white shark, *Carcharodon carcharias* from Australian waters, represent a hazard; killer whales, *Orcinus orca*, are also known to prey on leatherback turtles, the reptile's size being of little use against such fearsome predators.

Virtually nothing is known about the potential life span of these turtles, but for individuals that escape being hunted, it is thought to be measured in decades, as in the case of other sea turtles. While it is generally assumed that the leatherback turtle is solitary by nature, there have been accounts of sightings at sea of groups numbering as many as 100 individuals. Whether or not the groups are drawn together for mating purposes is unclear; it could simply be that they tend to congregate in areas where food is plentiful.

Freshwater Turtles

The freshwater turtles form the largest group of chelonians. They account for about 193 of the 238 species in the order Testudines, with representatives on all continents. They vary significantly in their habits: Some species are largely aquatic, leaving water only to lay their eggs, while others are primarily terrestrial, frequenting damp areas but able to swim as necessary. The shape of the carapace gives some indication of the turtle's lifestyle. For example, those with a streamlined, flatter shell, such as the softshell species in the genus *Trionyx*, are better suited to an aquatic existence than the box turtles, *Terrapene* species, whose shells are more domelike. In addition, long-necked turtles tend to have more difficulty walking on land compared with their short-necked relatives and so spend more time in water.

Common name Freshwater turtles **Order** Testudines

Family Carettochelyidae—1 genus, 1 species from Australia and New Guinea, the pig-nosed turtle, *Carettochelys insculpta*
Family Chelydridae—2 genera, 2 species of snapping turtles from North and Central America, including the common snapping turtle, *Chelydra serpentina*, and the alligator snapping turtle, *Macroclemys temminckii*
Family Dermatemydidae—1 genus, 1 species, the Central American river turtle, *Dermatemys mawii*
Family Emydidae—34 genera, 86 species of basking turtles from the Americas, Europe, and Asia, including the painted turtle, *Chrysemys picta*; pond slider, *Chrysemys scripta*; spotted turtle, *Clemmys guttata*; European pond turtle, *Emys orbicularis*; eastern box turtle, *Terrapene carolina*; Asian leaf turtle, *Cyclemys dentata*
Family Kinosternidae—4 genera, 21 species of American mud and musk turtles, including the yellow mud turtle, *Kinosternon flavescens*
Family Platysternidae—1 genus, 1 species from Southeast Asia, the big-headed turtle, *Platysternon megacephalum*
Family Trionychidae—5 genera, 23 species of softshell turtles from the Americas, Asia, and Africa, including the spiny softshell, *Apalone spinifera*
Family Chelidae—9 genera, 38 species of snake-necked turtles from the Americas, Asia, and Australia, including the oblong snake-necked turtle, *Chelodina oblonga*; matamata, *Chelus fimbriatus*; Krefft's river turtle, *Emydura krefftii*
Family Pelomedusidae—5 genera, 20 species of African and American side-necked turtles, including the pan-hinged terrapin, *Pelusios subniger*; yellow-spotted river turtle, *Podocnemis unifilis*

Many species of freshwater turtle are best described as semiaquatic. Although they live and feed in water, they will often emerge onto a rock or riverbank where they can bask in sunlight. This is especially true in more temperate areas, where the turtles generally leave the water toward midday. Basking allows them to raise their body temperature significantly although the water is relatively cold. They will then return to the water to look for food.

At night they remain submerged because that is when the air temperature drops more significantly than that of the water—they would experience too great a reduction in their own body temperature on land. In some areas turtles actually hibernate in the mud of their ponds over the winter period to avoid the cold. With their metabolism dramatically slowed down, they do not need to breathe so frequently and can often meet their respiratory needs through the direct interchange of oxygen and carbon dioxide in the water.

Taking in Heat

The shape and color of the carapace are important factors in determining the ability of turtles to absorb heat. Flat-shelled chelonians resting at the surface are better suited to absorb heat than those with more rounded shells, even if the latter emerge onto land. Dark-colored carapaces absorb and retain heat more effectively than pale shells. Basking on a rock is likely to raise the turtle's body temperature more quickly than emerging onto a riverbank. That is because the reptile can absorb the radiated heat given off from the rock into its body through the underside of the shell as well as the heat from the sun directly through the carapace.

Aquatic turtles have partially webbed feet to help in swimming, but they can also walk effectively on land.

↑ *Basking helps raise a turtle's body temperature. This red-bellied turtle,* Pseudemys nelsoni, *is basking and stretching itself on a log in Big Cypress National Park, Florida.*

→ *Feeding habits among freshwater turtles are varied. Some, such as the yellow-margined box turtle,* Cuora flavomarginata *from Southeast Asia, are omnivorous, eating flesh as well as fruits and leaves.*

Turtles that are typically found in ponds or other stretches of still water have relatively small feet compared with river turtles, which require more propulsive power when swimming against the current. Freshwater turtles can also use their feet rather like primitive hands to hold or break up food into pieces that can be swallowed more easily.

Freshwater turtles display a wide range of feeding preferences. Some species are largely herbivorous, while others are exclusively carnivorous, often hunting crustaceans and fish as well as scavenging occasionally on dead animals. The basic jaw structure of all freshwater turtles tends to be quite similar, with sharp cutting edges for seizing and biting off chunks of food. To make this process easier, some have a pronounced hook at the front of the jaws. They rely on scent and eyesight to detect their prey and alert them to danger, especially when out of the water.

A unique hunting behavior has been seen in the North American wood turtle, Clemmys insculpta. By making vibrations on the ground with its front feet, it causes earthworms to surface, earning itself a tasty meal.

Digestive Processes

The digestive system of freshwater turtles is similar to that of other chelonians, but there are key differences, mainly relating to the length of time food takes to move through the intestinal tract. They have a small tongue fixed to the floor of the mouth, which helps in swallowing; in a few sedentary species, such as the alligator snapping turtle, *Macroclemys temminckii*, there is a small projection on the tongue (known as a lure) that becomes bright pink when filled with blood and is used to attract prey. The esophagus is short and thin-walled, and takes food down to the stomach. From there it moves to the short intestine, where the actual digestive process begins.

Although digestion time is influenced by the temperature of the turtle's surroundings, it usually takes about four hours for food to leave the stomach. It may spend another 10 hours in the small intestine before moving into the large intestine, where it takes a further 20 hours to pass through. Waste matter is expelled from the body through the cloaca. Digestion in freshwater turtles typically takes far less time than in marine turtles or tortoises—in the case of the Aldabran tortoise, *Geochelone gigantea*, food can take up to 10 days to be completely digested.

A female arrau turtle, Podocnemis expansa, in the process of egg laying in Brazil. These turtles used to be common along riverbanks, but people who live near them relish the meat and also collect the eggs and even the hatchlings.

Breeding

Mating in freshwater turtles takes place in water. In many species there is a preliminary period of courtship, which can turn violent. The male will eventually grip the sides of the female's shell with his claws. He will also anchor onto her by biting on the folds of skin on her neck, although this causes no serious damage.

Female freshwater turtles emerge onto land to lay their eggs. The nest is covered and left unguarded. The young hatch after at least 30 days, but exactly when

Mating can be preceded by courtship, as in this pair of side-necked turtles, Emydura macquarii. At the surface the male bobs his heads and strokes the female's chin with his claws (1); under water the male strokes her head (2).

1

2

 SEE ALSO Turtle, Yellow Mud **47**:64

Prongs and Other Ploys to Avoid Predators

The semiaquatic cogwheel, or spiny turtle, *Heosemys spinosa*, is found close to forest streams throughout much of Southeast Asia. These turtles have a very distinctive appearance when they are young. Hatchlings have a decidedly rounded body shape with sharp projections running right around the edge of the carapace. It is thought that these prongs protect them from snakes, which are major predators in the areas where the turtles occur. As they grow older and larger, however, the prongs become far less evident. Another unusual feature of these turtles is the fact that, although they are essentially aquatic, they come onto land to seek fruit, which forms the basis of their diet.

Freshwater turtles head instinctively to water once they hatch, although they face a host of potential predators ranging from wading birds, such as herons, to fish and crocodilians. Both young and adults rely primarily on their speed and agility to escape predators.

Keen eyesight and smell also play a part in avoiding predators, and camouflage may also help on occasions. They can see well both above and below the water even into the distance. As a result, it is difficult to creep up on a basking turtle undetected. They also have good color vision, giving them an even clearer view of the world around them.

Some species have another way to deter predators. Notable examples are the musk turtles forming the American genus *Sternotherus* (family Kinosternidae). They reach a maximum adult size of only about 5.5 inches (14 cm). The common musk turtle, *S. odoratus*, is often described as the stinkpot because it produces an acrid yellowish secretion from special glands at the edge of the carapace. Most musk turtles can do this, and the secretion is thought to protect them from small carnivores. Once one of these predators tastes the foul discharge, it promptly drops the turtle.

depends partly on the species and partly on the ambient temperature. Freshwater turtles lay far fewer eggs in a clutch than their marine relatives, and mostly they do not appear to lay several times in succession during a season, although there is still a lot to learn about the individual habits of many species.

The breeding period is affected by climatic factors, notably temperature and rainfall. For example, species from North America lay during late spring, allowing their eggs to hatch well before the onset of winter, when the temperature can dip below freezing. In contrast, South American river turtles nest during the brief dry season, laying on the sandbanks. Therefore, while some species lay just once a year, others may lay several clutches in carefully chosen sites.

Female common mud turtles, *Kinosternon subrubrum* from the American Southeast including Florida, often lay their eggs in the nests made by alligators. This effectively guarantees them protection from predators, since the female alligator guards the nest site ferociously against would-be thieves.

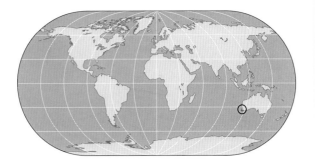

Common name Oblong snake-necked turtle

Scientific name *Chelodina oblonga*

Family Chelidae

Suborder Pleurodira

Order Testudines

Size Carapace at least 12.3 in (31 cm); up to 15.8 in (40 cm) according to some reports

Weight Approximately 3.3 lb (1.5 kg)

Key features Carapace has an oblong outline; neck when extended is virtually as long as the body and very muscular; color of the carapace very variable, ranging from dark fawn through blue-gray to black, occasionally dark brown with speckling; plastron bone-colored to brown; up to 12 tiny barbels (sensory projections) present under the chin; neck has a warty appearance; a dark band runs through the eyes; males tend to be slightly longer with a more concave plastron and a cloacal opening positioned farther back along the tail from the body

Habits Predatory by nature; sometimes wanders into gardens to nest

Breeding Female lays up to 156 eggs per clutch up to 3 times a year; eggs hatch after 30 weeks

Diet Carnivorous, hunting various invertebrates, amphibians, and fish; may also take small birds

Habitat Relatively slow-flowing rivers, lakes, and similar aquatic areas

Disribution Southwestern Australia

Status Does not appear under threat

Oblong Snake-Necked Turtle

Chelodina oblonga

Characterized by a neck that can be as long as its shell, the oblong snake-necked turtle is restricted to the Perth region of southwestern Australia. Females can sometimes be found wandering in backyards when looking for a place to lay their eggs.

THERE ARE APPROXIMATELY EIGHT recognized species of side-necked turtle, known as snake-necks, occurring in Australia. They all belong to the genus *Chelodina* and are characterized by having a combined head and neck length that is as long as the carapace.

Long Neck

The dark band running through the eyes of the oblong snake-necked turtle is unique. This species also has a proportionately longer neck than any other Australian member of the genus. Its neck is muscular to the extent that the turtle cannot withdraw it effectively by curling it under its shell. Probably as a result of this, these turtles can be aggressive, using the power in their neck to twist and turn with a view to biting a handler. When walking, the turtle is forced to hold its neck raised in a straight line in front of the shell.

Its long neck is an advantage in water, since it allows the turtle to lunge out at prey over a much wider area than would otherwise be possible. Its keen eyesight also enables it to strike under water with devastating effect. It is quite shy by nature, often frequenting areas of water where there are plenty of plants to provide cover. The turtle can then raise its long neck up to the surface to breathe while remaining for the most part concealed in the shallows.

Oblong snake-necked turtles mature at approximately half their adult size, usually about 6 inches (15 cm) in length. They may wander up to 546 yards (500 m) away from

⊖ **Unable to retract its long neck fully, the oblong snake-necked turtle curls it around the edge of the carapace.**

A Missing Link?

The oblong snake-necked turtle was discovered near Perth in southwestern Australia in 1839 by a local naturalist called John Gilbert. He arranged for the specimen that he had collected to be sent back to the British Museum in London, where it was described for the first time by the eminent herpetologist John Gray.

Unfortunately, a problem arose when the turtle was preserved for shipment back to England. The preservative method used resulted in its distinctive long neck being shortened to the extent that it became quite unlike that of a living specimen. This was to prove a serious cause of puzzlement for zoologists until the reason for the confusion eventually became clear.

water in order to nest. Females dig a hole about 7 inches (18 cm) deep, hollowing out the base to provide a chamber for the eggs. The digging can be completed in 15 minutes, and the female heads back to water within 40 minutes of starting the nesting process. The turtles are very conspicuous at this stage—near lakes around Perth in Western Australia signs are put up to warn drivers of the hazard of turtles lumbering across the road. This usually occurs any time from late afternoon until midnight during September to January.

The incubation period is quite long, usually lasting about 30 weeks. In some cases the young turtles remain in the nest site over the winter before finally emerging in spring. Their carapace is approximately 1.2 inches (3 cm) long at this stage.

Living in relatively shallow areas of water in some areas, the turtles may have to cope with pools that dry up in the summer. While some individuals move overland in search of other suitable habitats, others dig themselves into the drying mud and remain hidden there, only reemerging when the rains come again, possibly up to six months later.

Common name Matamata

Scientific name *Chelus fimbriatus*

Family	Chelidae
Suborder	Pleurodira
Order	Testudines
Size	Carapace 18 in (46 cm) long
Weight	33 lb (15 kg)

Key features Head very broad, flat, and triangular when seen from above; conspicuous skin flaps on head for detecting prey; nostrils protrude at the end of narrow tubes on the snout; eyes very small and positioned on top of the head; head coloration chestnut-brown above; throat reddish in hatchlings but variable in color in adults; young matamatas have a chestnut-red carapace, which is darker (almost black) in some adults; red plastron becomes brownish with age; small feet show little webbing; scales separated by areas of rough skin are evident on the limbs; tail short and tapering to a point

Habits Sedentary; hunts by ambush; almost entirely aquatic but not a powerful swimmer

Breeding Female lays clutch of about 20 almost spherical eggs with hard, calcareous shells; eggs can take about 30 weeks to hatch

Diet Small fish; possibly also crustaceans

Habitat Prefers calm waters such as lakes and ponds

Distribution Northern South America; widely distributed in suitable habitat throughout the Amazon basin

Status Not presumed endangered nor subject to heavy hunting pressure

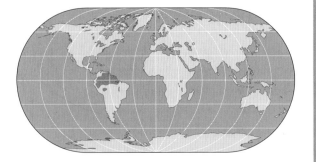

Matamata

Chelus fimbriatus

The highly distinctive profile of the matamata makes it one of the most instantly recognizable turtles in the world. Seen from above, young individuals look like fallen leaves.

THE BIZARRE APPEARANCE OF THE MATAMATA turtle does not serve only as camouflage—it is also significant in terms of the turtle's lifestyle. For example, the skin flaps on the matamata's head are important in helping it detect prey, since they are extremely responsive to the movement of fish and to vibrations in the water. In addition, the barbels in the throat area have a sensory function. Both the flaps and barbels themselves may even resemble edible items and therefore attract fish close to the turtle's head, where they can be snapped up.

Sensory Signals

Matamatas are sedentary predators. They wait for their prey to swim within reach rather than actively pursuing it, and therefore accurate sensory information is vital. Even when breathing, they do not surface—they simply extend their neck upward and rely on their snorkel-like nostrils to break the surface of the water in an inconspicuous fashion. The long nostrils can reach up more than 8 inches (20 cm) to the surface. Matamatas live in turbid water where visibility is poor, and so tactile senses are more significant than vision. This explains why their eyes are small. However, the tympanum on each side of the head is relatively large compared with other turtles. This has led to suggestions that sound transmitted in the water may also help the matamatas track the movement of possible prey.

As a target approaches, the matamata moves to extend its neck slowly and cautiously at first. It then allows the floor of its throat to expand very quickly, creating a current that literally sucks prey (such as fish) into its mouth. It then closes its mouth and forces out the

⊕ *Seen from above, the matamata's head is triangular with a long, slender snout. Its head and neck are covered in small skin flaps that move with the current, making the turtle look as if it were covered with weeds or algae.*

water before swallowing the fish. This technique is made possible by the development of the hyoid bones and associated muscles in the throat. The jaws themselves are actually quite weak and cannot be used to restrain prey. They have no tough horny edges, reflecting the fact that matamatas swallow their food whole rather than breaking off pieces.

Regional Variations

Matamatas are common in western areas of South America such as Colombia, but there are parts of the Amazon region, particularly in Surinam, where the turtles are either extremely rare or simply not present. However, the species can be regularly seen both in neighboring Guiana and French Guiana.

Since they occur over such a wide area, a number of supposed regional differences have been recorded in matamata populations. The divisions are based not just on coloration but are related to shell structure, notably in terms of the shape and size of the intergular scute (the

Seagoing Turtles?

Since the distribution of the matamatas extends right down to the mouth of the Amazon, there is the possibility that these turtles may also venture into brackish water occasionally. Although this has yet to be confirmed for this region, there is a record of an old matamata that was found alive on the southwestern coast of Trinidad. It had large, dead barnacles measuring up to 0.6 inches (1.5 cm) growing on its carapace. This shows that it must have spent considerable time in brackish surroundings and may even have been at sea. An established population of matamatas is found on Trinidad, which lies off the northern coast of South America. In addition, it is not uncommon for individuals that have been carried out to sea from the Orinoco River to end up on Trinidad, notably in the vicinity of the Nariva Swamp, augmenting the population there. This may well explain the origins of the beached matamata.

There is also a record of another matamata being caught farther east on a beach in French Guiana at the mouth of the Sinnamary River, suggesting that they may be carried down flooded rivers. Although they are not strong swimmers, these turtles can clearly survive drifting in flood water and may sometimes end up hundreds of miles from their place of origin as a result.

scute that divides the gular scutes at the front of the plastron). However, identifying individuals from particular areas by the variation in scute patterns may not be a reliable method—as more matamatas from the same region have been studied, patterning has not been found to be consistent within a single population.

Color is probably a more reliable indicator of origins, particularly in juveniles. Those from the Orinoco region, for example, have bright pink areas on the throat, often with small spots forming faint lines. In contrast, young matamatas from the Amazon itself display three alternating red and blackish bands across this part of the body. Shell shape is also a guide: Older specimens from this area tend to have slightly concave sides to the carapace, while in matamatas from the Orinoco the carapace is more convex. Males may grow slightly larger than females in all cases and have longer tails.

Lengthy Incubation

Relatively little is known about the breeding habits of these turtles. The nesting period seems to vary across their range. Because of the long incubation period (which has been

Rounding up the Fish

Studies of captive individuals have indicated that matamatas are resourceful and adaptable hunters. A group of three kept at the Bronx Zoo in New York apparently learned to drive fish that were provided for them as food into the shallow end of their pool. They used their legs to keep the fish from slipping back past them into deeper water. Although the technique was initially used by just one of the turtles, its companions soon adopted this approach as well.

A slightly different technique was observed in a group of matamatas at the Beardsley Zoological Gardens in Connecticut: Each matamata angled its body to corral the fish so they were within reach, while keeping the rear end of the shell uppermost. Although similar behavior has not been documented from the wild, it is tempting to think that these sedentary predators will use whatever technique is best suited to capturing their quarry, either encouraging fish into the shallows or up against an impenetrable barrier of reeds, where they can strike effectively at close quarters.

⊕ *The bright-pink throats of these two matamatas identify them as young individuals from the Orinoco region of South America.*

⊖ *Lying still on the bottom, the matamata waits for prey. Extending its long nostrils to the surface enables it to breathe without coming out of the water completely. Once the prey comes within range, the turtle uses its wide mouth and throat to suck it in.*

recorded as nearly 30 weeks) it tends to start early during the dry season. Instead of laying on sandbars, females usually haul themselves up riverbanks to dig their nests. They are thought to produce just a single clutch of eggs annually, and young matamatas probably reach sexual maturity at between five and seven years old.

Matamatas are generally not hunted for food throughout their range, apparently partly as a result of their rather grotesque appearance. Their anatomy is also quite different from other turtles found in this part of the world, and their small, weak limbs provide little meat.

What's in a Name ?

The origins of the unusual name of the matamata are unclear, although they probably reside in Brazil. It has been suggested that the name may be derived from the Tupi Indian word for "staircase," which refers to the steplike patterning of the dorsal scutes. Alternatively, it could be from the Arruan word meaning "skin," with the repetition in the name reinforcing the turtle's "fleshy" appearance. In Venezuela it is known as *la fea*, meaning "the ugly one."

Common name Krefft's
river turtle

Scientific name *Emydura krefftii*

Family Chelidae

Suborder Pleurodira

Order Testudines

Size Carapace up to 13.5 in (34 cm) long

Weight Approximately 2.75 lb (1.25 kg)

Key features Appearance varies across its range; head
larger in some populations than others; a
distinctive facial stripe extends back on each
side of the head from the eye to the rounded
area of skin at the side (which is the
tympanum); a narrow, bright yellow ring is
present around the pupil; iris is greenish in
some populations; there are tiny swellings
near the neck, but the head is covered in
smooth, gray skin; carapace is dark, varying
from shades of olive-green through brown to
blackish in some cases

Habits Fairly sedentary; can be seen basking on
riverbanks; may travel short distances
overland

Breeding Female typically lays 3 clutches at monthly
intervals, each with about 16 eggs; eggs
hatch after about 7–10 weeks

Diet Omnivorous; eats animal and vegetable
matter, including fruit and crustaceans

Habitat Mostly river and drainage systems; not usually
encountered in fast-flowing waters

Distribution Northeastern Australia ranging from Princess
Charlotte Bay as far south as Brisbane

Status Does not appear under threat

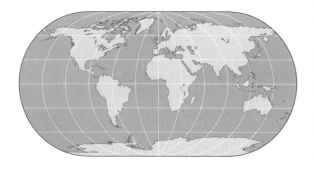

Krefft's River Turtle

Emydura krefftii

Krefft's river turtles are among the more common freshwater turtles in Australia and are sometimes seen in large numbers basking on riverbanks. However, they take to the water again at the slightest hint of danger.

THE NAME OF THIS TURTLE commemorates the achievements of Gerard Krefft, the German-born scientist who went to Australia during 1852 to seek his fortune in the gold fields but ended up being employed by the National Museum of Victoria. Credited with being the "father of Australian herpetology" for his pioneering work in the field, he was appointed director of the Australian Museum in Sydney in 1861. The turtle was named in his honor 10 years later.

Up to 70 million years ago side-necked turtles were widely distributed around the globe. Today they are restricted to the Southern Hemisphere. Although in parts of Africa and South America side-necked turtles and hidden-necked turtles (cryptodirans) are found together, all freshwater turtles in Australia belong to the suborder of side-necked turtles, Pleurodira.

Krefft's river turtle is a side-necked turtle, but it does not belong to the snake-necked group (which includes turtles such as the oblong snake-necked turtle, *Chelodina oblonga)*, whose members cannot retract their neck beneath their shell at all. It falls into the short-necked category (along with other *Emydura* species, such as the Brisbane short-necked turtle, *E. signata*). Its neck is withdrawn horizontally into the shell and is hidden under the overhang at the front of the carapace.

Regional Variations

In spite of its name, Krefft's river turtle actually prefers to inhabit lagoons and similar calm stretches of water rather than fast-flowing rivers in its range. There are distinctive forms throughout all the drainage systems where these turtles are encountered. In Queensland those found in the vicinity of the Endeavour River display grooving on the carapace, a feature shared with populations in the Burdekin River drainage system (also in Queensland).

A number of populations also have much broader heads than others, a characteristic known as macrocephaly. It is often a feature of older individuals in a population. The largest example on record had a skull measuring 2.2 inches (5.6 cm) in diameter at its broadest point across the tympanum. This may be a reflection of the turtles' feeding preferences in the areas concerned. For example, shellfish may figure more prominently in their diet, and they may therefore need more powerful jaw movements to crush the shells effectively. The appearance of these turtles changes in old age, however, with the carapace becoming more domelike in profile.

Rapid Reproduction

The courtship of Krefft's river turtles begins in April. But egg laying does not usually start until October, and continues until January. Hatching is relatively rapid, taking about seven weeks at a temperature of 86°F (30°C), although this period can sometimes extend to over 10 weeks depending on the prevailing conditions.

The young turtles measure just over 1.3 inches (3.2 cm) when they hatch. Hatchlings display a pale yellowish-white band around the carapace, and the vertebral scutes running down the center of the back have a slightly keeled appearance. The hatchlings will be sexually mature once they grow to a size of approximately 8 inches (20 cm). Both young and adults bask occasionally, but they remain very alert on land, slipping back into the water at the slightest hint of danger. They may, however, travel short distances overland, moving from one neighboring area of water to another.

They usually feed opportunistically, but there are indications that they tend to eat more plant matter once they are mature. They eat aquatic vegetation as well as fruits such as mulberries that fall from overhanging plants into the water. They in turn may be at risk of falling victim to crocodiles, which appear to be expanding their range in some parts of this river turtle's territory.

⊕ *This trio of Krefft's river turtles are sunning themselves by a pool in an Australian zoo.*

Common name Pan-hinged terrapin (East African black mud turtle)

Scientific name *Pelusios subniger*

Family   Pelomedusidae

Suborder   Pleurodira

Order   Testudines

Size   Carapace up to 8 in (20 cm) in length

Weight   Approximately 18 lb (0.8 kg)

Key features Shell relatively flat, smooth, and oval; body and head brownish to match shell; plastron hinged at the front; head large and brownish, occasionally marked with black spots; a pair of barbels normally present under the chin

Habits   Nocturnal; more likely to be active during the day in the rainy season

Breeding   Female lays about 8 eggs per clutch, possibly several times in the late summer; eggs usually hatch after 15 weeks

Diet   Omnivorous; eats plant and animal matter

Habitat   Stagnant areas of standing water such as ponds; sometimes found in sluggish streams

Distribution Tanzania and Burundi in East Africa southward to parts of the Democratic Republic of Congo, Botswana, and Zambia; found as far south as Mozambique and Kruger National Park, South Africa; also present on islands off the east coast, notably Madagascar, Seychelles, and Mauritius

Status   Does not appear endangered

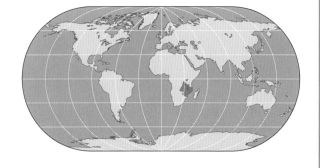

Pan-Hinged Terrapin

Pelusios subniger

The pan-hinged terrapin is a tropical mud turtle from eastern and southeastern Africa and Madagascar. Although it is a strong swimmer, it is usually found in shallow waters of marshes, streams, or ponds.

MEMBERS OF THE GENUS *PELUSIOS* are widely distributed across sub-Saharan Africa. Although the exact number of species is still being disputed, it is generally accepted that there are at least 14 in total. *Pelusios subniger* is known as the pan-hinged terrapin—its unusual name comes partly from its habitat and partly from its hinged plastron. These terrapins are often found in permanent bodies of water, although they are highly adaptable and can be seen in temporary pools of water following heavy rains, particularly in southern parts of their range. These areas are known locally as "pans." When the pools dry up, pan-hinged terrapins often burrow into the drying mud at the bottom and remain there until the rains come again, sometimes months later.

Disappearing behind the Hinge

In common with other members of its family, the pan-hinged turtle has a hinged flap toward the front of the plastron. It can withdraw rapidly into its shell and hide its head and front legs behind the flap. The muscle responsible for raising and lowering this flap is linked with those used for breathing. The front lobe of the plastron, which tends to be yellowish in color with a dark edge in this species, also tends to be bigger than the rear portion. This may give these relatively small terrapins some protection against crocodiles such as the widespread Nile crocodile, *Crocodylus niloticus*, that occur in various parts of their range.

The carapace is a uniform color, helping them blend in against the muddy base of stretches of water where they are encountered.

⊛ *Closely related to the pan-hinged terrapin, the West Africa black turtle,* Pelusios niger, *occurs on the other side of the continent. All members of the genus have relatively plain shell coloration.*

⊕ *A pan-hinged terrapin,* Pelusios subniger, *in Botswana. These small terrapins can hide their head and front legs behind their hinged plastron when danger threatens.*

In these places there is often algal growth on the shell, which also helps conceal their presence more effectively, although a typical pattern of growth rings can still be seen underneath. These rings do not correspond with an annual cycle that could enable the terrapins to be aged reliably—but they represent regular growth periods.

Distribution Patterns

Two distinct subspecies of pan-hinged terrapins have been identified. The mainland form, which is also present on Madagascar, is *P. subniger subniger,* while the race from the Seychelles is *P. s. parietalis.* The latter can be distinguished by the greatly enlarged size of its intergular scute. Two related members of the family—the African yellow-bellied mud turtle, *P. castanoides,* and the helmeted terrapin, *Pelomedusa subrufa*—found on the mainland also occur on Madagascar, and there is one endemic side-neck, the Malagasy big-headed turtle, *Erymnochelys madagascariensis.* It is clearly of older ancestral stock, since it has more in common with the side-necked turtles of South America, *Phrynops* species. However, a puzzle arises relating to the distribution patterns of *P. s. subniger* and

Other Mud Turtles

Widely distributed across the African continent south of the Sahara, the African mud turtles have colonized a diverse range of habitats. Some have proved to be highly adaptable. For example, the helmeted terrapin, *Pelomedusa subrufa*, is often encountered in arid areas. It frequents temporary pools, sometimes burying itself as the water evaporates and remaining concealed until the rains return. Its versatility extends to its diet as well—these terrapins have even been seen feeding on the ticks of rhinoceroses that come to wallow in the water.

Larger marsh terrapins actively hunt birds, such as doves, that are attracted to waterholes to drink. They catch them unawares and drag them below the surface, where they drown them, using a hunting technique similar to that adopted by crocodilians. The shells of these particular side-necks are quite thin, however, and they themselves would be no match for crocodiles. That is perhaps why they frequent shallow, temporary waters, where they are unlikely to run into crocodiles. Adept at moving overland when necessary, these terrapins are often killed as they attempt to cross roads in search of new aquatic habitats.

In contrast, the much larger serrated hinged terrapin, *Pelusios sinuatus*, which can attain a carapace size of over 18 inches (46 cm), lives in permanent stretches of water and scavenges on the remains of game killed by crocodiles. Neither its serrated shell nor its extra size guarantee it protection from the crocodiles, however.

Other members of this group of side-necked turtles have become more specialized in their habits, notably the African forest terrapin, *Pelusios gabonensis*. It is found in rain-forest areas on the continent, living in fast-flowing streams. Some species have very restricted areas of distribution, as typified by Broadley's mud terrapin, *Pelusios broadleyi*, whose range is limited to northern Kenya along the southeastern shore of Lake Rudolph. Another localized species is the Okavango hinged terrapin, *Pelusios bechuanicus*. It is found predominantly in the deep water of the Okavango swamp in Botswana, where it hunts both fish and invertebrates.

E. madagascariensis: Rather than being located on the west coast of Madagascar nearest the mainland, the pan-hinged terrapin is confined to the eastern side of the island, while the big-headed turtle occurs in the west. It is possible that the pan-hinged terrapin was introduced there by settlers or traders from Africa. The reptiles of Madagascar have evolved independently to the extent that many species occur nowhere else, and the presence of this species on both Madagascar and the mainland therefore suggests that its arrival on the island was quite recent.

The pan-hinged terrapin is also well established on the Seychelles along with the yellow-bellied terrapin, *P. castanoides*, and an endemic side-neck, the Seychelles mud terrapin, *P. seychellensis*. The latter may be extinct, but there is no evidence that the introduced terrapins have contributed to its decline.

 SEE ALSO Crocodilians 47:94

Nevertheless, pan-hinged terrapins do have a reputation for being highly aggressive toward other turtles. Therefore this may have been a significant factor if the adults of *P. s. parietalis* had resorted to attacking hatchlings of their relative on the Seychelles.

On Mauritius it is thought that the introduced population of pan-hinged terrapins may have died out already. There are other accounts of this species occurring on Glorioso Islands as well as Diego Garcia, which forms part of the Chagos Archipelago. Although they may be exposed to brackish water conditions in some parts of their range, there is no real evidence that these small chelonians would be able to spread to places throughout the Indian Ocean without human assistance.

Opportunistic Feeders

Pan-hinged terrapins are highly adaptable in their feeding habits, eating both plants and aquatic creatures ranging from snails and crabs to small fish. Mainly nocturnal by nature, these terrapins are more likely to become active during the day in the rainy season. They take a wide range of prey and are opportunistic feeders. They have been reported to attack creatures much larger than themselves, including birds.

The nesting period generally starts in February or March, although this varies depending on location. Females probably lay two or three clutches in succession with an interval of several weeks between them. A typical clutch consists of between eight and 12 relatively small eggs that average about 1.4 inches (3.6 cm) in length. The incubation period usually lasts for about 15 weeks at 86°F (30°C). The young terrapins are approximately 1.3 inches (3.5 cm) long when they hatch, and they weigh about 0.27 ounces (7.6 g).

⊕ *Pelusios sinuatus* *from tropical East Africa is the largest hinged terrapin. It is known as the serrated hinged terrapin because it has a sharply defined black pattern around the edge of its shell.*

Common name
Yellow-spotted
river turtle

Scientific name *Podocnemis unifilis*

Family   Pelomedusidae

Suborder   Pleurodira

Order   Testudines

Size   Carapace can reach 27 in (69 cm) long

Weight   20 lb (9 kg)

Key features Carapace has a convex shape most apparent in juveniles; 2nd and 3rd vertebral scutes slightly keeled; color ranges from dark brown to black; yellow to orange spots on head; front lobe of the plastron is shorter and wider than the rear lobe, and is a lighter buff-gray color in juveniles but grayer in adults (often with black markings); irises in females are blackish but green in males and juveniles; adult females also differ from males by a lack of head spots; those in males disappear by the time they reach maturity; females generally grow to a larger overall size

Habits   Highly aquatic but may occasionally bask, typically in groups

Breeding   Females lay 15–40 eggs in a clutch depending on location; eggs hatch after 63 days

Diet   Predominantly, but not exclusively, herbivorous; eats aquatic plants and snails

Habitat   Rivers, lakes; avoids fast-flowing water

Distribution Colombia eastward throughout the Amazon basin, including the Orinoco, extending as far south as parts of Bolivia and Brazil

Status   Vulnerable (IUCN) because of hunting pressure

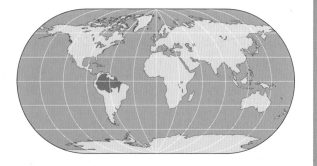

Yellow-Spotted River Turtle

Podocnemis unifilis

The yellow-spotted river turtle is not the biggest river turtle in South America, but it is one of the most heavily hunted. Both its meat and eggs are eaten, and attempts to protect the turtle are largely ineffective.

THE STRIKING SPOTS ON THE HEAD that give these turtles their common name are most evident in young hatchlings, although the spots are not always yellow—they can be orangish in some cases—and they are more distinctive in some parts of the turtle's range than others. The scientific name *unifilis* refers to the presence of just one barbel on the throat. While this is a fairly consistent feature in yellow-spotted turtles originating from the Orinoco River, elsewhere it appears to be more variable, and some populations have paired barbels.

Yellow-spotted turtles are most likely to be seen in rivers and lakes, although they tend to avoid fast-flowing stretches of water. In the wet season, therefore, they are likely to venture into the *llanos* (flooded forest areas) rather than remain in rivers that are swollen by torrential

floodwater. At this time they may feed more extensively on fruits that fall into the water, although at other times they tend to browse on aquatic plants such as water hyacinth, *Eichornia*, as well as eating aquatic snails.

In calm areas of water the yellow-spotted river turtle has an unusual way of feeding: by filtering plant matter at the surface. The turtle opens its mouth and swims with its lower jaw just below the waterline. When it breaks the surface, water floods down into its throat, carrying any edible matter with it. The turtle then forces the water out of its mouth through its jaws, using its pharynx. The solid matter stays in its throat and is then swallowed.

Breeding begins at the start of the dry season. The female turtles emerge onto the sandbanks to bask at intervals before they begin to lay their eggs. The males, distinguishable by their smaller size and more colorful appearance, remain in the water, where mating occurs. The nest site is located at the highest point on the beach about 130 feet (40 m) from the water, and the females emerge under cover of darkness to lay their eggs. The eggs are hard shelled and decidedly elongate in shape. Once the clutch is complete, the female buries the eggs using her hind feet, hiding them beneath about 4.8 inches (12 cm) of sand. The process takes about two and a half hours on average; when it is finished, she returns immediately to the water. The young turtles hatch after approximately 63 days.

Hunting Pressure

Unfortunately, the nests are often raided before the end of the incubation period by local people as well as other predators, including tegu lizards, *Tupinambis* species, and birds such as crested caracaras, *Polyborus planus*. With a reputation for making good eating, the turtles are still heavily hunted for meat despite the fact that they are protected in much of their range. Enforcement is difficult to achieve. Furthermore, since numbers of the larger South American river turtle (or arrau), *P. expansa*, have declined sharply in many areas because of overexploitation, hunters have switched their attention to the yellow-spotted river turtles. In Venezuela they are sometimes caught during the wet season on hooks baited with plantain. They are occasionally speared when they come to the surface to breathe as well as being trapped in nets.

⊕ *A group of yellow-spotted river turtles compete for space on a log in the Amazon region of Ecuador.*

Common name Alligator snapping turtle

Scientific name *Macroclemys temminckii*

Family Chelydridae

Suborder Cryptodira

Order Testudines

Size Carapace about 26 in (66 cm) in length

Weight 219 lb (99.5 kg)

Key features Head large; jaws prominent and hooked; tail long; carapace varies in color from brown to gray depending on the individual and has 3 distinctive keels arranged in ridges, resembling those on the back of an alligator; feet on all four limbs end in sharp claws; lure present in mouth to attract prey

Habits Sedentary predator usually found in deep stretches of water; lures prey within reach especially during the daytime; may become more active as a hunter at night; strictly aquatic, but females leave the water to lay their eggs; relatively weak swimmer

Breeding Occurs in spring and early summer; clutches contain up to 50 eggs that hatch after about 100 days

Diet Eats anything it can catch, including birds, small mammals, other turtles, fish, and mussels where available; also eats fruit and nuts

Habitat Relatively sluggish stretches of water

Distribution North America from Kansas, Illinois, and Indiana to the Gulf of Mexico, including Florida and eastern Texas

Status Declining; now rare in many parts of its range; protected locally in parts of United States; Vulnerable (IUCN)

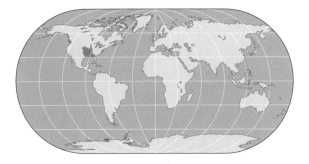

Alligator Snapping Turtle

Macroclemys temminckii

The alligator snapping turtle ranks among the largest of all freshwater turtles, as well as being the biggest found in the United States. However, giant specimens are very rarely encountered these days.

ALLIGATOR SNAPPING TURTLES get their common name from the keeled ridges on their carapace, which resembles the back of an alligator. They used to be heavily hunted to make turtle soup, which was a popular dish in the southern states. During a three-year period in the mid-1980s more than 37,736 pounds (17,117 kg) of their meat was bought by a single dealer in Louisiana. Even today hunting is a potential problem in some areas, and habitat change has generally had a harmful effect on the populations of alligator snapping turtles.

An exception has occurred in Florida, however, as a result of drainage of the Apalachicola River. The silt that was dredged out of the river was deposited on the floodplain. Clutches laid there by alligator snapping turtles were subsequently exposed to raised temperatures during the incubation period, giving rise to a higher percentage of female offspring among the hatchlings.

This occurred as a result of temperature-dependent sex determination (TDSD), in which ambient temperature during incubation plays an important part in determining the sex of the developing young. The extra females should help increase the reproductive potential of the species in this area, since a greater number of females in the population will mean that more eggs are laid.

Luring Prey

The alligator snapping turtle's bulky body means that it is not well suited to being an active predator. As a result, the species has developed a very distinctive method of obtaining prey.

 SEE ALSO Turtles 47:8; Freshwater Turtles 47:28; Turtle, Common Snapping 47:52

⊕ The alligator snapping turtle is unusual in being able to pump blood to its tongue, creating a lure to entice fish into its mouth. It feeds mainly on fish but will also capture and eat small turtles.

These turtles are well camouflaged in their surroundings thanks in part to their dark coloration, and they often feed during the day. An individual will rest in a characteristic hunting pose on the muddy bottom with its mouth open. A projection on its tongue turns pink as it fills with blood and acts as a lure to entice prey into its jaws. The turtle can even move this structure to make it look like a wriggling worm. As soon as the prey enters its mouth, the turtle snaps shut its jaws. At other times, however, the lure is relatively inconspicuous and whitish in color, drained of blood and lying on the floor of the mouth.

This method of feeding is especially common in juvenile alligator snapping turtles. As they grow older, their feeding preferences and tastes change. It has been suggested that the main type of food in the diet of these turtles was once freshwater mussels; but thanks to the effects of water pollution and overexploitation of stocks the mussels have become rare, and the turtles have been forced to switch to other food. In areas where the mussels are available, however, they feature significantly in the turtles' diet.

Their powerful jaws also enable them to feed on smaller turtles occurring in their habitat, such as the common musk turtle, *Sternotherus odoratus*, and even their smaller relative, the common snapping turtle, *Chelydra serpentina*. There is virtually nothing that large alligator snapping turtles will not prey on—they eat all types of creatures, including birds such as wood ducks, *Aix sponsa*, and even mammals such as raccoons, which they seize in their massive jaws. The turtle drags them under water and drowns them before eating them.

The alligator snapping turtle is not exclusively predatory by nature, however. It has a keen sense of smell, which makes it an effective scavenger. One turtle was even trained to find human corpses in the waterways of Indiana. It was released on a wire leash into the water close to where a person had disappeared, and it was followed by observers in a boat as it picked up the corpse's scent. It also feeds opportunistically on vegetable matter such as persimmons and acorns, gathering these seasonal foods as they fall

47

from trees and bushes overhanging the water—acorns in particular form a significant part of the turtle's diet in some places.

Breeding Behavior

The mating period of alligator snapping turtles begins in February and usually lasts until April. Where several males congregate hoping to mate with a single female, they often behave aggressively toward their potential rivals in an attempt to drive them away. A male that wants to mate with a female first sniffs her body carefully starting in the vicinity of her head. He then moves down the side of her body to the cloaca before mounting her under water. He grips her with his claws, anchoring on slightly to one side of her body. This enables him to direct his tail beneath the female's so that he can introduce his sperm into her body.

As in many other chelonians, the gap between the base of the tail and the opening in the anogenital region is longer in males, which aids mating. Copulation itself can last anywhere from five to 25 minutes, with the male

she can deposit her eggs. It seems that the number laid depends to a significant extent on the size of the female, with larger individuals laying comparatively bigger clutches of up to 50 eggs. The eggs themselves are hard shelled and relatively spherical in shape.

The nests of alligator snapping turtles can sometimes be raided by predators like raccoons. It typically takes about 100 days or so for the eggs to hatch. The carapace of the hatchlings measures about 1.8 inches (4.6 cm) in length at this stage.

Mossbacks

Although alligator snapping turtles naturally inhabit rivers in the Mississippi drainage area of southern parts of the United States, they are relatively weak swimmers. They prefer to move by walking on the riverbed. They do not come onto land to bask, yet the heavy growth of green algae present on the carapace of many larger individuals suggests that they regularly spend time in shallow areas of water. Relatively intense sunlight falling on their backs is responsible for triggering the development of the plant growth, and it may even spread farther along the upper surfaces of the head and tail in some cases. As a result, the turtles are often referred to as "mossbacks" by people in the Deep South.

A dense covering of algae (not, in fact, moss as suggested by its nickname) often coats the shells of alligator snapping turtles that frequent shallow waters.

releasing a steady stream of air bubbles out of his nose during this period.

When she is ready to lay, the female alligator snapping turtle hauls herself onto land and digs a nesting chamber with her hind feet. This activity often takes place during the day. The nest is enlarged at the base to accommodate the eggs. It may extend over 12 inches (30 cm) down into the ground.

The female starts by digging a pit into which she can lower much of her body. She then creates a smaller hole beneath, into which

Giants of the Past

Although there are only two surviving species in the family
Chelydridae (the other being the snapping turtle, *Chelydra
serpentina* from Canada to Ecuador), snapping turtles used to be
much more widely distributed, including in Europe. Another species
of alligator snapping turtle, *Macroclemys schmidti*, lived in North
America about 26 million years ago near present-day South Dakota.
Records suggest that the largest alligator snapping turtles were found
in northern parts of the species' range, possibly migrating there from
farther south. It is also likely that much larger specimens than those
officially known to zoologists existed.

One of the most celebrated "giants" was the so-called "Beast of
Busco," or Oscar, as it became known. It was originally reported by a
farmer in the summer of 1948. He spotted the monstrous turtle in
Fulk's Lake, a stretch of water covering some 7 acres (2.8 ha) near
the town of Churubusco in Indiana. It was seen again in March
1949, and some townsfolk made an attempt to corral the turtle in a
small area of the lake. They constructed a stockade using stakes and
managed to keep the giant reptile confined in 20 feet (6 m) of water.
Unfortunately, it managed to break out of the enclosure. Those who
observed the turtle said that it was about the same size as a dinner
table, with a heavy covering of algal growth on its back. Its weight
was estimated as being about 500 pounds (227 kg). A film of the
event was taken at the time but has subsequently been lost.

More than 200 witnesses saw the turtle try to seize a duck that
was being used as a lure to catch it. It was then decided to drain the
lake to expose the "Beast of Busco," but the attempt nearly ended in
tragedy when two people became trapped in the treacherous mud
that coats the bottom of the deep lake and almost drowned. After
that the turtle was left alone, and nothing more appears to have
been written about it. However, the story has been immortalized in a
unique annual turtle festival held in the town that takes place during
June. It lasts for four days and includes a carnival parade as well as
turtle racing, and now even the town's official logo features a turtle!

Other myths surround these turtles, not least that their jaws are
reputed to be strong enough to break a broom handle with a single
bite. Tests have shown that even a large alligator snapping turtle
weighing 40 pounds (18 kg) would have difficulty snapping a pencil
in this way, although the shearing effects of the jaws are such that
they can bite chunks out of boats when lifted aboard. Big specimens
are very dangerous to handle not just because of their strong jaws
but because of their powerful flippers, which have sharp claws.

Once they are in the water, the young
turtles may occasionally fall victim to larger
individuals of their own species, but they are
more likely to be caught and eaten by
alligators. While these turtles will prey on small
gars, *Lepisosteus* species, larger examples of
these fish, which can reach 10 feet (3 m) in
length, regularly hunt small alligator snapping
turtles in return.

Forced to Move

There is some evidence that alligator snapping turtles are territorial. Established individuals may actively resent the incursion of smaller turtles into their territory. This may be related to the fact that the turtles can be forced to shift regularly from one locality to another in order to guarantee a food supply. In some areas at least it appears that the lure in their mouth often becomes less effective at attracting prey over the course of several years, and fish tend to avoid it. This may be particularly significant in view of the fact that these turtles are potentially very long-lived. There are reliable records of individual alligator snapping turtles in zoological collections living for over 60 years, and it is thought that their life expectancy could be much longer, possibly more than 100 years.

↑ *Twenty-one years after it was stolen from a reptile park, this 110-pound (50-kg) alligator snapping turtle was found in sewers in Sydney, Australia. It has since been returned to the park.*

Common name Common
      snapping turtle

Scientific name *Chelydra serpentina*

Family   Chelydridae

Suborder   Cryptodira

Order   Testudines

Size   Carapace length up to 24 in (61 cm)

Weight   Up to 82 lb (37.2 kg)

Key features Head powerful; jaw hooked; barbels
      present on lower jaw with small tubercles on
      the neck and underparts; eyes prominently
      located near the snout; carapace brown and
      relatively smooth in older individuals but with
      a more pronounced keel in younger turtles;
      plastron relatively small in area with no
      patterning and varies from whitish to coppery
      brown; tail quite long with a crest running
      down the upper surface

Habits   Relatively shy; spends long periods concealed
      in mud or vegetation; usually more active at
      night; often rests during the day, floating just
      under the surface with the eyes protruding

Breeding   Female lays single clutch of 25–80 eggs (but
      may lay more than once a year); eggs hatch
      after minimum of 2 months

Diet   Predominantly carnivorous; eats fish,
      amphibians, other turtles, birds, snakes, and
      small mammals; also eats plant matter

Habitat   Occurs in virtually any type of standing or
      flowing fresh water, especially where there is
      a muddy base and vegetation

Distribution Southern parts of Canada through the
      United States and Central America south to
      Ecuador

Status   Reasonably common

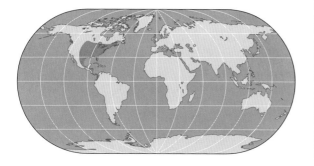

Common Snapping Turtle

Chelydra serpentina

Although it does not grow as large as its relative, the alligator snapping turtle, Macroclemys temminckii, *the snapping turtle is a voracious predator. It has powerful jaws that can inflict a painful, damaging bite.*

THERE IS SOME DISPUTE over the taxonomy of the snapping turtle. Its range extends from southern parts of Canada through the United States and Central America as far south as Ecuador. Although it is traditionally divided into four subspecies within this range, DNA studies have led to the suggestion that the population should be split into two or three distinct species, with those in southern areas being recognized as separate from the northern populations. In the east the Florida snapping turtle, *C. s. osceola*, is also considered to be a separate species by some taxonomists. It is restricted entirely to the Florida peninsula but appears to differ little from examples occurring elsewhere in North America.

Musky Females

The mating period of snapping turtles varies from April to November in different parts of their range. It is thought that females emit a pheromone from a gland in the cloaca that attracts males when they are ready to mate. The secretion has a distinctive, musklike odor. Courtship is aggressive: The male pursues the female, snapping initially at her head and legs to slow her down. If she accepts his advances, she raises her hindquarters, and both turtles then face each other for a period, while moving their head from side to side. The male then moves around the female's body and climbs on top of her, anchoring himself with his feet. Mating lasts for about 10 minutes.

Female common snapping turtles do not need to mate every year in order to lay fertile eggs. In common with many other chelonians females are able to store viable sperm in their reproductive tract from previous matings, which will fertilize future egg clutches. As a result, the eggs laid by a female of this species can produce hatchlings of different parentages.

Nesting begins in May, peaks in June, and can continue until as late as September. A rise in air temperature above 50°F (10°C), especially in combination with some rain, triggers nesting behavior. Egg laying begins either at dusk or dawn. Larger females tend to nest earlier in the season and lay proportionately more eggs in a clutch than younger individuals laying for the first time.

Dug in a wide variety of soil conditions usually in the open and often some distance from water, the nests themselves are vulnerable to predators, including skunks and raccoons. Some snakes, notably the eastern king snake, *Lampropeltis getulus getulus*, will also eat turtle eggs readily. Often what happens is that eggs at the top of the nest are destroyed

⬅ *Female snapping turtles make a bowl-shaped cavity in loose sand, loam, or plant debris. In the nest the eggs are vulnerable to predators, and this female in Ohio takes no chances and stays close by.*

➡ *An average of 40 eggs are laid, and incubation lasts at least two months. The young emerge from the nest and head for water, where they hide under cover from predators.*

as a result of predation, but those at the bottom survive and hatch.

The incubation period tends to vary markedly through the snapping turtle's range. Eggs hatch after just two months in warm surroundings but take much longer in northern parts, where the young may even overwinter in the nest before emerging the following spring. If the nest is shallow, however, they may be killed by frost over this period. The young hatchlings emerge under cover of darkness and are directed toward the water by the light reflecting off its surface. (Marine turtle hatchlings, notably loggerhead turtles, *Caretta caretta*, use a similar method of finding their way to the sea.)

Predators and Prey

Common snapping turtles measure about 1 inch (2.5 cm) when they hatch, and their long, flexible tail is similar in length to their shell. They may use the tail as an anchor at first, clasping onto vegetation to keep themselves from being swept away by the current once they enter the water.

They spend much of their early life concealed in these surroundings, often lying partly hidden in the streambed to avoid drawing attention to themselves. This is a particularly dangerous time for the young turtles—they face many predators, from wading birds such as herons to amphibians such as large bullfrogs, *Rana catesbeiana*.

Young snapping turtles have voracious appetites of their own, however, enabling them to grow rapidly. Males eventually reach a larger size than females. Both sexes are sexually mature once their carapace has grown to about 8 inches (20 cm) long, by which time they are between five and six years old. Their growth then slows significantly. Other changes in appearance are evident as they grow: The shell becomes relatively long compared with its width, and the tail is proportionately shorter compared with their overall size.

Their hunting habits also tend to change as they grow older, with mammals and birds more

likely to fall prey to them at this stage. Muskrats, for example, may be seized and dragged under water. They are held under until they drown and are then eaten. Adult ducks may suffer a similar fate. Larger individuals have even been seen preying on smaller members of their own kind, and carrion also features in their diet. But even adult snapping turtles are not entirely safe from predators, particularly in southeastern parts of the United States, where their distribution overlaps with that of the American alligator, *Alligator mississippiensis*. These large reptiles will eat the whole turtle, including the shell, which is crushed in their powerful jaws.

Snapping turtles are also hunted on a wide scale for their meat. The equivalent of over 6,000 adults were caught commercially in Minnesota in the late 1980s, for example, and 8,000 in southern Ontario. Regulations are in force to regulate this trade, certainly in the northern part of the species' range, but trade in the subspecies *C. s. rossignonii* from Central America and *C. s. acutirostris* from South America is less well documented and could be endangering these populations.

Nasty Bite

Estimating numbers of snapping turtles in a given area is not easy because they are less inclined to enter baited traps than other turtles whose range overlaps with theirs. Handling common snapping turtles is not straightforward either, since they can be a genuine danger to the unwary. While most turtles can be safely held by the sides of their shells, common snapping turtles are able to reach around with their head and inflict a serious bite. They are highly aggressive when restrained, and the safest way to move an individual is by grasping the upper and lower ends of the carapace and holding it away from your body.

Few turtles occur in such a wide range of aquatic habitats as the common snapping turtles. They can be found anywhere from muddy pools to fast-flowing rivers and readily move across land if food becomes short, or if

water levels fall significantly. They often travel under cover of darkness, when they are naturally more active. During the day they often rest by floating just under the water's surface with their eyes protruding, keeping a watch on their surroundings. As a result, their shell develops a covering of green algae, which helps conceal their presence even more.

They rarely bask on land, however, unless plagued by leeches. In that case they are forced to dry off in order to make the parasites dehydrate and let go. Their disinclination to bask is probably related to the relatively large amount of water they lose from their body when on land as well as to their dislike of high temperatures.

During the winter, however, individuals in northern areas will hibernate in the mud on the bottom of a river or pond. They dig themselves in usually by the end of October and then emerge the following March. In areas closer to the equator the turtles may bury themselves in mud and wait for the rains to return if the pools in which they are living dry up. While common snapping turtles are essentially found only in fresh water throughout their range, on rare occasions they can be encountered in brackish areas.

Not afraid to tackle even venomous prey, a snapping turtle eats a rattlesnake, Crotalus viridis.

Common name Big-headed turtle

Scientific name *Platysternon megacephalum*

Family   Platysternidae

Suborder   Cryptodira

Order   Testudines

Size   Carapace up to 8 in (20 cm) long

Weight   Approximately 2.2 lb (1 kg)

Key features Head massive, its width sometimes half the length of the carapace; skull covered in a thick, bony casing; jaws powerful with a hook at the tip; top of head protected by a single horny scute extending down behind the eyes; carapace relatively flat and brownish with variable blackish markings and a central ridge running down its length; tail long, almost as long as the carapace when curled back; plastron light brown with a variable blackish patterning

Habits   Nocturnal; very aggressive; can often be encountered on land as well as in water

Breeding   Female lays small clutches of just 1 or 2 eggs; hatching time about 2–3 months

Diet   Fish and various invertebrates; may venture onto land to feed

Habitat   Fast-flowing mountain streams

Distribution Southeastern parts of Asia

Status   Endangered (IUCN); listed on CITES Appendix II

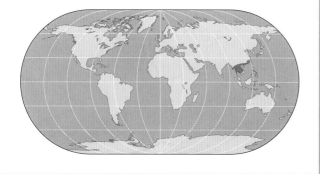

Big-Headed Turtle

Platysternon megacephalum

Well (if not elegantly) named, the big-headed turtle from Southeast Asia is unlike any other turtle. Its most striking feature is the triangular head, which can be almost half as wide as the carapace.

THE HIGHLY DISTINCTIVE BIG-HEADED TURTLE is the only member of its family. Its anatomy and biology are so unusual that it appears to have no close relatives. It has been suggested that it could be a distant relative of the New World snapping turtles in the family Chelydridae (in spite of the vast difference in size), but it appears that any similarity is more the result of convergent evolution than of a genetic relationship.

The turtle's wide, triangular-shaped head is so large that it cannot be withdrawn beneath the carapace. Instead, it relies for protection on the horny scute on its skull and its ability to bite ferociously if attacked or handled. This behavior is common in species that cannot protect themselves by withdrawing into their shell.

Tree Turtle?

Another unusual feature of the big-headed turtle is its long, muscular tail, which enables it to climb very effectively by helping with balance and providing anchorage. Although the head is heavily armored, the bridges at the sides of the shell are surprisingly flexible, giving the turtle greater freedom of movement when climbing.

Although they occur in the tropics, big-headed turtles are found at quite high altitudes and are therefore adapted to living in relatively cool surroundings. The streams that they inhabit are fast flowing but shallow. As a result, they tend to move by walking over the bottom rather than swimming. This may also keep them from being swept away in the current. They tend to seek out overhangs and places under the water where they can retreat to avoid the strongest currents.

Human Enemies

Like many Southeast Asian chelonians, the big-headed turtles appear to have declined dramatically in numbers over recent years. Although there are plenty of areas of suitable habitat remaining in central and southern parts of China as well as elsewhere within their range, these turtles have been heavily collected for sale in the food markets within the region—demand for turtle meat has grown significantly over recent years.

Growing affluence in some parts of Asia has actually resulted in increased demand for traditional foods such as turtles, and this marks the start of a cycle. As species become rarer, the price increases, and this can actually result in increased demand. Conservation measures are very hard to enforce. Although the

Convention on International Trade in Endangered Species (CITES) should help prevent unauthorized movement of the species across borders in the region, policing is unreliable, and the convention gives no protection in terms of the domestic use of wildlife.

The case of the big-headed turtle is especially worrying because of its low reproductive rate. Females may lay no more than one or two eggs a year, which makes them among the least fecund of all the world's chelonians. Damage to breeding stocks today will be hard to reverse in the future even with the help of captive-breeding programs, making the prospects particularly bleak for this turtle. There is also some harm being caused to its habitat by the construction of small hydroelectric plants.

In Hong Kong populations of the big-headed turtle appear to have declined less than in China itself, and the turtle remains reasonably widespread throughout central and eastern parts of the New Territory; it is also found on Lantau Island west of Hong Kong Island.

Elsewhere in its range nothing is known about the population in Myanmar, but in Laos and Vietnam collecting is believed to have increased over recent years, and the species is endangered in both countries. In Thailand much of the range of the big-headed turtles lies in northern areas of hill forest that are largely protected by local government; in some areas they are not uncommon, although it is suspected that some smuggling of the turtles still goes on.

Because the head of the big-headed turtle is too large to be pulled back beneath the shell, it has extra protection in the form of a large horny scute on its head.

Common name Pig-nosed turtle
(pitted-shelled turtle)

Scientific name *Carettochelys insculpta*

Family   Carettochelyidae

Suborder   Cryptodira

Order   Testudines

Size   Carapace up to 22 in (56 cm) in the case of
the New Guinea population

Weight   Up to 50 lb (22.5 kg)

Key features Broad front flippers and paddlelike hind
legs make it look like a sea turtle; number of
claws is also reduced to 2 on each limb;
snout highly distinctive and piglike, almost
resembling a small trunk; thin skin covering
the shell is pitted, accounting for its
alternative common name of pitted-
shelled turtle

Habits   Highly aquatic; only females come onto land
to breed; often remain still under water to
avoid being seen

Breeding   Australian females lay 7–19 eggs in a single
clutch each year; eggs take at least 70 days
to hatch

Diet   Omnivorous; feeds on fruit such as figs,
vegetation, and invertebrates such as
crustaceans and mollusks

Habitat   Relatively shallow, slow-flowing stretches of
water

Distribution Southern New Guinea; Northern Territory in
Australia

Status   Has declined in some parts of New Guinea
over recent years; Australian population
appears stable; Vulnerable (IUCN)

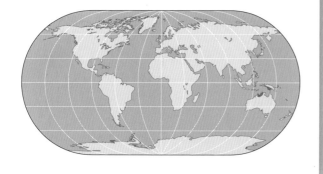

Pig-Nosed Turtle

Carettochelys insculpta

*The pig-nosed turtle is undoubtedly one of
the strangest-looking turtles in the world.
Unlike any other freshwater turtle, it has
paddlelike flippers resembling those
of marine turtles.*

THE CARETTOCHELYIDAE IS A FAMILY whose ancestral
line extends back over 40 million years. Its
members were more widely distributed in the
past, and their fossilized remains have been
discovered in parts of Asia and Europe as well
as North America. Today, however, the pig-
nosed turtle is the sole survivor. Apart from a
population in the north of Australia it is
confined to southern New Guinea. Perhaps
surprisingly, its presence in Australia's Northern
Territory was not confirmed until 1970 in spite
of Aboriginal rock art dating back over 7,000
years that portrays these distinctive turtles in
the region. Its discovery came after a fisherman
caught a turtle on the Daly River. Investigations
revealed that a previously unidentified clutch of
turtle eggs dug up from the East Alligator River
in 1924 also belonged to this species.

The Great Divide

It is thought that the population of pig-nosed
turtles divided when the landmasses of New
Guinea and Australia separated. As a result of
the split there are now some differences
between the two groups of pig-nosed turtles
today, with those found farther north in New
Guinea growing to a larger size than their
Australian relatives. Both are effectively isolated
because, in spite of some similarities to sea
turtles, it appears that pig-nosed turtles cannot
survive in the marine environment. However, in
parts of their range in New Guinea they can
sometimes be encountered in brackish water.

Pig-nosed turtles are mainly vegetarian in
their feeding habits. They use their claws to tear

⊕ *The snout of the
aptly named pig-nosed
turtle can be seen clearly
from the front. Also
visible are the forelimbs,
which are highly
modified into
flipper-shaped blades,
making the turtle a
superb swimmer.*

Hunting and Habitat Damage

Not a lot is known about the New Guinea population of these turtles, although it is clear that in some areas they have been heavily hunted. This has led to a reduction in their numbers. Although protected in Australia, there are fears that introduced water buffalo, *Bubalus bubalus*, now living in a feral state, are damaging the nesting habitat of the turtles with their hooves by churning up the areas where the turtles lay their eggs.

apart aquatic vegetation to make it easier to swallow. Their short neck means that it would be hard for them to lunge at prey. Under water they prefer to conceal their presence by remaining hidden and motionless if possible; but if disturbed, their powerful flippers allow them to escape very quickly, which may give some protection against attacks by crocodiles.

It is thought that groups of pig-nosed turtles come together for mating purposes during June and July. Female pig-nosed turtles often show signs of scarring on their face caused by the male's claws during mating encounters.

Egg laying in Australia's Daly River region, where the country's largest population occurs, takes place in the dry season and lasts until November. The eggs hatch after about 10 weeks. Both the eggs and the hatchlings tend to be smaller than those laid in New Guinea. The young turtles emerge during the rainy season and sometimes stay in the nest until the rains come. Conditions during the incubation period determine the gender of the hatchlings

(a process known as TDSD, or temperature-dependent sex determination). The critical temperature for the pig-nosed turtle's eggs is 87°F (31.5°C). Above this female hatchlings will result; at a lower temperature the hatchlings will be mainly male. Hatchlings have a distinctive low keel running down the center of their back and serrations around the edges of the shell.

The young turtles probably spend the early months of their life seeking food across the floodplains rather than in the swollen rivers. Their rate of growth is relatively slow, with both sexes only becoming sexually mature once they have attained a carapace length of 12 inches (30 cm), which is likely to take at least 15 years.

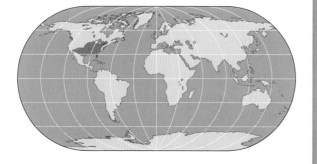

Common name Spiny
softshell

Scientific name *Apalone spinifera*

Family   Trionychidae

Suborder   Cryptodira

Order   Testudines

Size   Carapace length 6.5 in (16.5 cm) to 18 in
               (46 cm) in females; from 5 in (13 cm) to
               9.3 in (23.5 cm) in males

Weight   Approximately 2.2 lb (1 kg) to 3.3 lb (1.5 kg)

Key features Flattened, leathery shell lacks scutes and is
               circular; underlying color varies from olive to
               tan; patterning highly variable; spots (ocelli)
               on carapace have black edges; distinctive
               spiny tubercles on the front edge of shell are
               unique to this species; neck long with dark-
               edged lighter stripes; nostrils elongated and
               snorkel-like; limbs powerful and paddlelike

Habits   Fast swimmer; predominantly aquatic but will
               emerge to bask on occasions; burrows into
               mud or sand beneath the water to hide with
               just the head exposed

Breeding   Female lays 4–32 white, spherical eggs; eggs
               probably hatch after about 8–10 weeks

Diet   Carnivorous; eats mainly invertebrates such as
               crayfish; larger individuals may take fish and
               amphibians

Habitat   Still or slow-flowing waters that are often
               shallow with sandy or muddy bottom; may
               also occur in faster-flowing waters

Distribution North America from southern Canada south
               across the southern United States, including
               the Florida Peninsula, and around the Gulf
               Coast in Mexico

Status   Generally quite common

Spiny Softshell

*Apalone
spinifera*

*The highly aquatic spiny softshells seldom venture out
of water except to bask. The Latin name* spinifera
*means "bearing thorns," a reference to the spinelike
tubercles on the carapace edge just behind the head.*

MEMBERS OF THE FAMILY TRIONYCHIDAE, to which the
spiny softshell belongs, are widespread. They
occur in parts of Africa and Asia as well as
North America. The spiny softshell is one of the
most widely distributed species. Its range
extends from southern parts of Canada across
much of the southern United States and south
as far as Mexico.

Six distinctive subspecies have been
identified. The eastern softshell, *Apalone
spinifera spiniferus*, is relatively large with black
borders around the spots (ocelli) on the
carapace. In contrast, the western race,
A. s. hartwegi, has much smaller ocelli as well
as dots on its carapace. Unlike these two forms,
the Gulf Coast spiny softshell, *A. s. asper*, has
at least two lines at the rear of the carapace.
The Texas race, *A. s emoryi*, has a pale rim to its
carapace, which is much wider along the rear
edge, and there are also white tubercles present
on the rear third of the carapace. In the pallid
subspecies, *A. s. pallidus* from west of the
Mississippi and east of the Brazos River, the
tubercles are more prominent, extending over
the back half of the carapace. In the case of the
Guadalupe spiny softshell, *A. s. guadalupensis*,
the white tubercles cover most of the carapace
and are encircled by black rings. In places where
two different races overlap, however, they can
be difficult to distinguish because they show
characteristics of both populations.

Pancake Turtles

Turtles in this family are sometimes known as
pancake turtles due to their flat, circular shape.
Spiny softshell turtles are adept at burrowing in
mud or sand beneath the water, hiding away
and leaving just their head exposed above the

surface. They do not need to surface in order to breathe as frequently as other turtles, since they can absorb oxygen directly in the pharyngeal region of their throat as well as through their leathery shell. In extreme cases they are able to remain under the water for up to five hours. During the winter period in northern parts of their range they will hibernate in the water by burying themselves under several inches of mud. During this time they slow down their respiratory rate.

Mating occurs in the spring, and egg laying peaks during June and July. Females haul themselves onto land and dig a nest site quite rapidly using their hind feet. They sometimes complete this task in under 15 minutes.

It is not uncommon for the nesting turtles to empty their bladder

⊕ *A female spiny softshell basks at the side of a river with its head raised, revealing the unusual long, piglike nose that is characteristic of the species.*

into the hole as they dig to make the soil particles stick together and help the excavation process. They invariably choose a sunny site close to water.

Young spiny softshells start to emerge from the end of August through to October, but in the far north of their range the young may overwinter in the nest, emerging for the first time the following spring. They measure about 1.4 inches (3.6 cm). They appear to be relatively slow growing and only reach sexual maturity when they are about 10 years of age.

The species is known for its longevity—the largest females can be over 50 years old. They face relatively few threats except for pollution of the water, which can be a major hazard in some areas. Adults are sometimes caught for food, but generally these softshells are not subjected to heavy hunting pressure.

Their powerful feet mean that the spiny softshells are able to live in fast-flowing rivers but are equally at home in ditches. When seeking food, they often prefer to comb the bottom rather than swim actively in search of prey. Invertebrates such as crayfish are their main prey items, but larger individuals also prey on fish and amphibians, notably frogs.

Central American River Turtle

Dermatemys mawii

Common name Central American river turtle

Scientific name *Dermatemys mawii*

Family Dermatemydidae

Suborder Cryptodira

Order Testudines

Size Carapace up to 26 in (66 cm) long

Weight Up to 48.5 lb (22 kg)

Key features Carapace flattish, olive green in color with a thin covering of scutes that are easily damaged but with a well-developed bony skeleton beneath; feet powerful and webbed to aid swimming; head small relative to largish body size

Habits Highly aquatic; spends much of the time floating near the surface of the water

Breeding Female may lay 2 clutches a year averaging 6–20 eggs in total

Diet Mainly herbivorous; eats fruit and aquatic plants

Habitat Found in rivers and also calmer, large areas of water including lakes and lagoons

Distribution Central America from the Atlantic lowland region of southern Mexico (Veracruz, Campeche, Chiapas) into northern parts of Guatemala and Belize; an isolated population in Honduras

Status Endangered (IUCN); protected locally

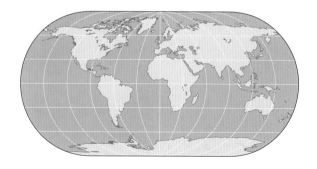

Dermatemys mawii is a nocturnal aquatic turtle that lives in larger rivers and lakes in Central America from southern Mexico to northern Honduras.

THE CENTRAL AMERICAN RIVER TURTLE is the only member of its family and appears to be the sole survivor of an ancient lineage of turtles believed to have originated over 70 million years ago in Asia. From there the group spread across to Europe and Africa in the west and to the Americas; since then both its range and numbers have declined dramatically.

The species became known for a time as the Tabasco turtle after it was discovered in this Mexican state in 1847, but its range is now known to be more extensive. As its name suggests, it is confined to parts of Central America from the Atlantic lowland region of southern Mexico (the states of Veracruz, Campeche, and Chiapas) across the border into northern parts of Guatemala and Belize. It is possible that the species once ranged over an even wider area of Central America, since an isolated population has been recorded farther south in northwestern Honduras.

Despite being relatively large, Central American turtles are hard to observe because of their highly aquatic nature. They do not emerge onto rocks or the riverbank to bask but prefer to float near the surface. This allows them to retreat rapidly into the depths if they are disturbed without drawing attention to their presence. Central American river turtles graze on aquatic plants and also feed on fruit that drops into the water.

Breeding in the Wet

These turtles are not well equipped to walk on land. They have difficulty even raising their head in such surroundings; as a result, they have evolved a very unusual breeding strategy. Unlike most river turtles that occur in parts of Central and southern America, they do not nest during the dry season when the river level is low and exposed sandbanks are available briefly for nesting purposes. Instead, Central American river turtles breed at the peak of the rainy season, when the rivers are in full flood. This means that they can swim away from the main river into side tributaries, which they would otherwise be unable to reach.

Females simply need to move a short distance out of the water to lay their eggs, typically choosing a site within 5 feet (1.5 m) of the water's edge. There is then less risk that the nest itself will become flooded, and the shallow side channels that are left once the floodwaters recede serve as a better nursery for the young turtles than the river itself. If the nest does become flooded, however, the eggs

Although its head is relatively small, the Central American river turtle has a large, slightly upturned nose. It is shaped like a tube with wide nostrils and projects forward strongly from the front of the head.

can survive being submerged for up to a month after laying without any adverse effects on the numbers that will hatch.

When the young emerge and head to the shallows, it should be reasonably easy to find food in the channels. They will also be in less danger from the river otters that prey on these turtles in deeper water.

The shell of the Central American river turtle is deceptively strong, however, and provides some protection against predators. Although the scutes overlaying the shell are thin and can be quite easily damaged or worn down, the bony layer beneath is surprisingly thick. As the sutures (the lines that join the sections) in the bone disappear in older individuals, it forms an almost solid casing.

Hunting Pressure

In some parts of their range Central American river turtles may inhabit estuarine waters, since they have been found with barnacles on their shells. What is perhaps more unusual given their inability to walk on land is their presence in *aguadas*, which are seasonal pools often located well away from other stretches of water in Guatemala. It may be that they become trapped there as the dry season advances, or they may have been left by human hunters, secure in the knowledge that they would still be there when they returned.

Unfortunately, populations of Central American river turtles have declined significantly over recent years because of intense hunting pressure. They are known in Spanish as *tortuga blanca*, meaning "white turtle," and are highly valued for their meat. This has led to the turtles becoming almost extinct in some parts of the region. However, in order to safeguard the future of the species, there are now protective regulations in place throughout their range.

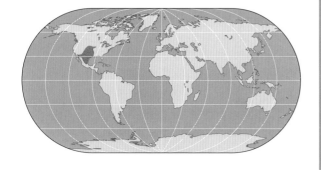

Common name
Yellow mud turtle

Scientific name *Kinosternon flavescens*

Family	Kinosternidae
Suborder	Cryptodira
Order	Testudines
Size	Length of carapace 6.3 in (16 cm) maximum
Weight	Approximately 1.3 lb (0.6 kg)
Key features	Carapace predominantly olive-brown and smooth with an oval shape; yellow coloration confined largely to the jaw and throat area, including the 2 barbels on the chin; plastron relatively large and light brown in color (darker in some individuals than others) with distinct hinges at either end; males have a concave plastron and patches of scales on the inner side of the hind legs; tail long, ending in a spiny tip
Habits	Spends daytime in water, often emerging to feed on land at night; most active during June and July
Breeding	Female typically lays 1 clutch containing 4 eggs, but numbers vary from 1–6 in total; eggs hatch after about 75 days
Diet	Omnivorous; eats mainly aquatic invertebrates; on land eats snails and other terrestrial invertebrates
Habitat	Slow-flowing streams and similar stretches of fresh water, especially where there is plenty of aquatic vegetation
Distribution	Central and southern United States to Mexico
Status	Reasonably common, although the subspecies *K. f. spooneri* is regarded as State Endangered in Illinois, Iowa, and Missouri

Yellow Mud Turtle

Kinosternon flavescens

The common name of the yellow mud turtle comes from the yellow areas on its throat, head, and neck. The plastron has two hinges, allowing the turtle to retreat into its shell and seal each end separately.

MUD TURTLES ARE WIDELY DISTRIBUTED throughout northern and central parts of America, extending down to Colombia in South America. The yellow mud turtle occurs in central parts of the United States from northern Nebraska south to Texas. It can be distinguished in all cases by the presence of an elevated ninth marginal scute. Its range also covers parts of New Mexico and southeastern Arizona extending across the Mexican border.

Several distinctive subspecies are recognized throughout its range. The most northerly form, *Kinosternon flavescens flavescens*, also displays the most pronounced yellow coloration, which extends onto its carapace. The Mexican form, *K. f. stejnegeri*, has an olive carapace with a particularly long gular scute compared with the front lobe of the plastron. The dark-shelled Illinois yellow mud turtle, *K. f. spooneri*, is the rarest subspecies, and its existence is threatened largely by the effects of water pollution. It occurs in the northwest of Illinois and adjacent parts of Iowa and Missouri. Habitat conservation will be vital in the future to ensure its continued survival.

Yellow mud turtles can be found in a wide range of aquatic environments, including both natural and artificial areas of calm water, ranging from swamps to sinkholes and even cattle troughs. They are often seen basking during the day, especially when the weather is warm and sunny. Their level of activity varies through the year, however. It peaks during June and July, when they are active during the day, particularly in the late afternoon, and at night. They feed largely on the bottom and rely on

⊕ *The scorpion mud turtle, Kinosternon scorpoides from Costa Rica, is related to the yellow mud turtle. However, its carapace is slightly more domed.*

their keen sense of smell to locate edible items, sometimes even scavenging on carrion. Occasionally they also feed on land.

Breeding takes place during July and August. They have sometimes been seen mating out of the water. The hard-shelled eggs are buried—females occasionally lay them in heaps of vegetation rather than straight into the ground. The raised temperature resulting from the decomposition of the plant matter may help speed up the development of the embryos. Unlike many chelonians, female yellow mud turtles prefer to start digging their nest hole using their front feet at first, completing the task with their hind legs.

The eggs usually take about 75 days to hatch, and the young measure approximately 1.2 inches (3 cm) when they emerge. Young Illinois yellow mud turtles are quite different compared with the adults and display a series of pale spots on their chin and a dark shell.

⬆ *Yellow mud turtles frequent small bodies of water that can dry up in summer. They spend the cooler months under leaf litter, in tree stumps or muskrat dens, or buried in mud under water.*

All yellow mud turtles grow quite slowly. As a result, males are unlikely to breed for the first time until they are at least four years old, and the females are usually slightly older.

Digging in for the Winter

As the fall advances in the northern parts of their range, the mud turtles often emerge onto land to find suitable areas for hibernation. They may dig themselves in under logs or burrow straight into the soil. They may invade muskrat dens. Since they often occur in areas of water surrounded by open woodland, these turtles may even hibernate in old tree stumps on occasions as well.

Yellow mud turtles are most likely to be encountered on land when it is raining or soon afterward. During dry periods they prefer to immerse themselves in standing areas of water.

Adults face relatively few predators, possibly because they have scent glands that give off a repellent smell if they are directly threatened. In addition, the yellow mud turtles can seal themselves into their shell thanks to two hinges on the plastron. They prefer to defend themselves in this way rather than by attempting to bite. The young are more at risk of predation, however, because of their small size. This makes them vulnerable to various predatory fish, for example, as well as other reptiles, including snakes.

Common name Painted turtle

Scientific name *Chrysemys picta*

Family Emydidae

Suborder Cryptodira

Order Testudines

Size Carapace up to 10 in (25 cm) long

Weight Approximately 2.2 lb (1 kg)

Key features Shell smooth with no keel or serrations along the rear of the carapace; in eastern painted turtle the central vertebral shields and adjacent side shields are aligned rather than overlapping; different subspecies identified easily by distinctive coloring and patterning; pattern of yellow stripes on head, becoming reddish on the sides of head and front legs; females grow larger than males; males have longer front claws than females

Habits Semiaquatic; often leaves the water to bask

Breeding Female may produce clutches of anything from 2 to 20 eggs; eggs hatch after 10–11 weeks on average

Diet Young tend to be carnivorous; mature painted turtles eat a higher percentage of aquatic vegetation

Habitat Relatively tranquil stretches of water, ranging from smaller streams to lakes and rivers; eastern form occasionally found in brackish water

Distribution Central and eastern parts of North America from Canada in the north to Mexico in the south

Status Relatively common

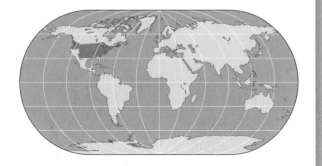

Painted Turtle

Chrysemys picta

The painted turtle is the most widely distributed North American turtle and the only one whose range extends across the entire continent. Because of their size and attractive colors painted turtles are often kept as pets.

PAINTED TURTLES GET THEIR NAME from their bright coloration. Four distinct subspecies are recognized through their range. The eastern painted turtle, *Chrysemys picta picta*, occurs farthest east and is found from southeastern Canada down the Eastern Seaboard of the United States to northern Georgia and Alabama. A particular feature of this subspecies, which makes it virtually unique, is the way in which the central vertebral shields running down the back and the adjacent shields on either side are aligned rather than overlapping. This creates a distinctive pattern of lines running across the shell.

The eastern painted turtle can also be identified easily by its unmarked yellow plastron. This helps distinguish it from the midland painted turtle, *C. p. marginata*, which also has a blackish carapace but has a dark patch at the center of the plastron. This feature is apparent even in young hatchlings, although the exact pattern of markings on the underside of the shell differs according to the individual. As its name suggests, the range of this subspecies lies to the west of its near relative, extending across Canada from southern Quebec to Ontario and occurring as far south as Oklahoma and Alabama.

The southern painted turtle, *C. p. dorsalis*, is perhaps the most distinctive subspecies of all thanks to the yellow or sometimes reddish stripe that runs down the center of the carapace. The plastron is yellowish in color with no markings. As its name suggests, its range does not extend as far north as Canada; it is confined to the United States from southern Illinois southward to the Gulf of Mexico, ranging from Oklahoma to Alabama.

⬇ *The eastern painted turtle,* Chrysemys picta picta, *has a greenish carapace with thick lines between the aligned scutes and red markings around the edge. The plastron is yellow.*

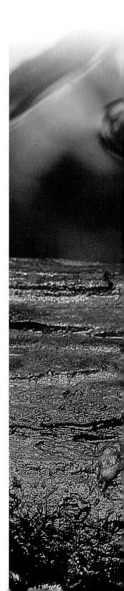

The western painted turtle, *C. p. belli*, occurs farther west. It is found over a wider area than the other subspecies. It ranges farther north into British Columbia as well and is found in a number of localities in the southwestern United States—it even occurs in an area in Chihuahua, Mexico. It has distinctive lines over the carapace as well as elaborate patterning that extends to the edge of the plastron. It has potentially the largest size of all the subspecies. Where the different races of painted turtle overlap, however, they interbreed, giving rise to offspring with intermediate characteristics. This is known as intergradation.

Courtship and Breeding

Courtship begins in April. At this stage the reason for the male's longer front claws becomes apparent. He swims up in front of a female, approaching her headfirst. He gently uses his claws to fan water close to her face and then starts to touch her face. Assuming she is receptive, she responds by

touching his face. The pair then swim to the bottom. The male grips onto the female, placing his legs at each corner of her shell, and mating takes place. A pair may remained joined in this way for up to 15 minutes.

The nesting period itself usually extends from May to July. Females typically emerge from the water to lay either soon after dawn or in the late afternoon. To make digging easier, they

⊕ **Chrysemys picta belli,** *the western painted turtle, is the most widespread of the four subspecies and grows to a larger size than the others—up to 10 inches (25 cm).*

choose a site that has soft soil, often moving up onto a bank or even near a road, where the area is unlikely to become flooded. The nest itself is usually quite shallow, often less than 4 inches (10 cm) deep.

In northern parts female painted turtles tend to lay only once or twice during this period. Farther south they can lay throughout the season and produce up to four clutches. There are differences among the subspecies as well, with the relatively large western painted turtle producing more eggs per clutch than the southern race, which is the smallest. In any population large females invariably lay more eggs compared with smaller individuals. Breeding is unlikely to occur until the female is six years old; in some areas females may not lay every year if the temperature is too cold.

How Did the Subspecies Evolve?

There is a tendency to think that species are created as individual populations become isolated. However, this process can occur in reverse, which may be true in the case of the painted turtle. It is believed that at the time of the last Ice Age (about 18,000 years ago), today's painted turtles existed as three separate species. Their distribution was somewhat similar to their current ranges, except that they did not extend as far north because of the presence of the ice sheet.

The western painted turtle was present in the Southwest, and the southern painted turtle was confined in the vicinity of the lower Mississippi region. As the climate warmed, it is thought that these two distinct populations followed the retreating glaciers northward. They met around what is now known as the Missouri River, and thus began a process of hybridization that ultimately resulted in the development of the midland painted turtle.

In turn the midland painted turtles traveled northward as far as the eastern area of the Great Lakes. Sandwiched between their two ancestral forms, they occupied the area where they are found today. The movement of the eastern painted turtle up the Atlantic coast also resulted in contact with the southern painted turtle on the western side of its distribution. Instead of remaining isolated, therefore, the three original species came together, with the result that the painted turtle now enjoys the widest distribution of any aquatic chelonian on the North American continent.

The time taken for the eggs to hatch varies depending on local conditions, but incubation usually takes between 65 and 80 days. The gender of the offspring is determined by the temperature at which the eggs hatch—at higher temperatures of about 87°F (30.5°C) females are produced, but at temperatures below 77°F (25°C) males develop. It is unclear whether the female is influenced in this respect when choosing her nesting site. Young painted turtles have a rounded carapace. They are little more than 1 inch (2.5 cm) in length, but they grow fast at first, doubling their size within a year. This makes them less vulnerable to the many predators that they face when young.

Basking in Groups

It is quite common to see painted turtles basking out of water, often with their hind legs stretched out behind them. This helps keep

⊕ Although they spend most of the time in water, painted turtles often sun themselves on a log, a rock, or the shore. They are often seen in large groups.

⊕ The different subspecies of painted turtles are distinctive. This is a southern painted turtle, C. picta dorsalis, distinguished by a reddish-orange stripe running down the center of the carapace.

their shells healthy and raises their body temperature. In some areas it is not uncommon for up to 50 turtles to share a partially submerged rock or log when basking, often lying on top of each other. This may make them less vulnerable to predators—if one individual detects possible danger and dives back into the water, all the others will follow very rapidly.

Painted turtles display a regular daily routine, emerging to bask early in the morning. This means that they can raise their body temperature and therefore their level of activity at this stage, plunging back into the water to feed before basking again in the early afternoon. They then look for more food and finally burrow into the bottom of their stream or pond overnight.

Basking is particularly significant in temperate areas because, even if the water temperature is relatively low, the turtles can take advantage of any additional warmth provided by the sun. Painted turtles may enter a dormant period in northern parts of their range during the winter months; but although they become sluggish, they may not be completely inactive—they have been seen swimming even in ice-covered water. Their body temperature under these circumstances has been shown to be higher than that of their surroundings, suggesting that they have a primitive mechanism for heat regulation.

Common name Pond slider

Scientific name *Chrysemys scripta*

Family   Emydidae

Suborder   Cryptodira

Order   Testudines

Size   Varies from 8.3 in (21 cm) to 24 in (60 cm) depending on subspecies; females in all cases grow larger than males

Weight   Approximately 2.2 lb (1 kg) to 4.4 lb (2 kg)

Key features Vary with subspecies; the well-known red-eared slider (*T. s. elegans*) has distinctive red flashes on either side of the head behind the eyes, which are pale green with a dark horizontal stripe; body has a striped pattern consisting of yellow and green markings; carapace greenish with darker markings, especially in older individuals; plastron yellowish with individual dark markings

Habits   Semiaquatic; emerges regularly to bask

Breeding   Female lays 12–15 eggs in a clutch, often nesting several times in a season; eggs hatch after 6–10 weeks on average

Diet   Invertebrates, including tadpoles and aquatic snails; small fish; adults also eat plant matter

Habitat   Slow-flowing stretches of water with plenty of vegetation

Distribution North, Central, and South America

Status   Relatively common

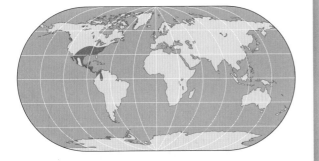

Pond Slider

Chrysemys scripta

Pond sliders love to bask on logs or rocks near water. Sometimes two or three can be seen piled on top of each other. "Slider" describes the way they retreat quietly into the water at the slightest threat.

NO OTHER SPECIES OF TURTLE is so variable in appearance throughout its range as the pond slider, whose distribution extends from southeastern Virginia in the United States south through Mexico as far as Brazil. There are 14 distinctive subspecies recognized over this area, of which the red-eared slider, *Chrysemys scripta elegans*, is by far the best known thanks to its popularity in the pet trade. Its natural range extends through the Mississippi Valley from the Gulf of Mexico up to Illinois.

Large numbers of hatchlings were once exported to Europe. However, fears that unwanted pets dumped in waterways could prove harmful to native wildlife led to an importation ban by the European Community in 1997. Nevertheless, red-eared sliders are still being bred commercially in the United States and also now on a large scale in parts of the Far East, where most are sold for food rather than as pets. This may help protect native Asiatic turtles, which have been subjected to heavy hunting pressures over recent years.

Riverine Life

The name "slider" refers to the way in which the turtles slip into the water if disturbed while basking. In southern parts of their range they are more commonly seen in river habitats.

Breeding behavior varies according to location. In temperate areas females lay in the early summer, typically between April and July. Courtship varies markedly among the different subspecies depending on whether or not the males have elongated claws on their front feet. Where they are present, as in the red-eared slider, the male approaches his intended mate from the front, fanning her face with water and

⊕ *The red-eared slider,* Chrysemys scripta elegans, *can be distinguished from all other North American turtles by the presence of a broad red stripe behind the eye.*

using his claws to stroke her face. In the case of the Mexican race, *T. s. taylori*, however, males adopt a more aggressive style of courtship. They simply bite at the rear of the female's shell and snap at her legs. It is possible that the female releases a particular scent when she is receptive, which may trigger this behavior.

In South America, where pond sliders occur more often in rivers, nesting habits are less influenced by temperature than by rainfall. Egg laying in this region tends to occur during the dry season, when the sandbars are exposed. The young turtles take from about six to nine weeks to hatch and have a circular shape when they first emerge from the egg. They also tend to be more brightly marked on the carapace than adults, in which the patterning becomes obscured with age.

Color Changes

Older male pond sliders can end up being almost black. This phenomenon is known as acquired melanism because of the increased presence of the black pigment melanin in the shell of older individuals. (This process is a little like hair turning gray with age.) Other types of color change can be found in these turtles.

Occasionally what are known as leucistic slider hatchlings are recorded. They are the result of a genetic mutation that causes them to have no melanin, a characteristic that can be passed from one generation to the next. Their entire body and shell tend to be a muddy yellow color overall, and the distinctive color flash on the head of most sliders appears paler than normal in these mutated individuals.

Young sliders are highly carnivorous at first, and the relatively large percentage of animal protein in their diet fuels their fast growth. They prey on a variety of small aquatic creatures ranging from tadpoles to aquatic snails and small fish. Once they are older, however, pond sliders tend to eat more plant matter and become omnivorous in their feeding habits.

European Pond Turtle

Emys orbicularis

Although its appearance varies over its large range, the European pond turtle is often identifiable by the bright yellow or gold speckling on its dark carapace and skin.

Common name European pond turtle

Scientific name *Emys orbicularis*

Family   Emydidae

Suborder   Cryptodira

Order   Testudines

Size   Carapace from 5 in (13 cm) to 7 in (18 cm) long

Weight   Approximately 1.8 lb (0.8 kg)

Key features Carapace relatively low and flattened; coloration varies but usually consists of a dark background with yellow markings in the form of streaks or spots; head coloration blackish with yellow spots; tail in males longer than in females; males also have a slightly concave plastron and red rather than yellow eyes; females larger on average than males

Habits   Semiaquatic; will emerge to bask, but behavior varies throughout its wide range

Breeding   Mating takes place under water; female lays clutch of 3–16 eggs (with an average of 9) on land; eggs usually hatch after about 70 days

Diet   Aquatic invertebrates and fish; adults tend to eat more plant matter

Habitat   Relatively sluggish stretches of water as well as ponds

Distribution Europe from Lithuania and Poland in the north across most of southern Europe and into North Africa and west to Turkmenistan

Status   Declining in many areas because of pollution and habitat modification; Lower Risk (IUCN)

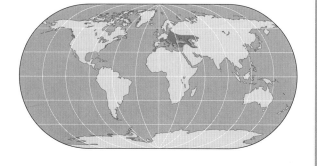

THE EUROPEAN POND TURTLE is the only freshwater turtle to be found throughout much of Europe. These chelonians have a more restricted range than they did in the geological past, however. They once reached Scandinavia and parts of England, but they died out there about 5,000 years ago. Several attempts to reintroduce them to the British Isles in Victorian times failed, indicating that climatic changes were probably responsible for their demise.

Their distribution still extends over a wide area ranging from Lithuania and Poland in the north and then across most of southern Europe and into North Africa along the Mediterranean shore from Morocco to Tunisia. Unfortunately, European pond turtles are becoming much rarer in many areas, particularly in agricultural regions of France and Italy, as a result of loss of habitat, including the concreting of drainage ditches. They are adaptable, however, and in some areas they have colonized artificial stretches of water.

European pond turtles favor waters where there is a muddy base combined with plenty of aquatic vegetation, which provides them with plenty of retreats. They prefer slow-flowing or even still areas of water and are sometimes found in marshland. On a few occasions they have been recorded in brackish areas as well.

Multiple Subspecies

Owing to the fact that they occur over such a wide area, there are marked variations in the appearance of the turtles throughout their range. Taxonomists tend to recognize 13 different subspecies grouped across five geographical ranges. There are also noticeable

Conservation Success

A detailed study of European pond turtles in Spain has confirmed that the species has declined markedly—in many cases because of the effects of water pollution. Existing populations soon become isolated and gradually decline in number. Then they fail to breed, usually as a consequence of habitat changes along the waterways where the turtles live.

However, careful conservation measures can lead to a significant increase in numbers where suitable protected habitat is available. In parts of Catalonia in the northeast of Spain conservation efforts increased the local population of pond turtles from barely 40 to over 300 during the course of about 10 years.

differences among the groups in terms of breeding habits. Breeding times extend from March through June but start later in northern latitudes. It is thought that, at least in some parts of their range, these turtles vocalize when seeking a mate, uttering brief calls. Males chase after a potential mate, bumping her shell and biting at her legs from behind to slow her down before climbing on top of her carapace. Mating occurs under water, and the female lays her eggs on land between four and six weeks later. Clutches consist of about three to 16 eggs, the average being nine—larger females produce bigger clutches. The eggs themselves have leathery rather than hard shells.

The incubation temperature is critical to the development of the hatchlings and determines what sex they will be. (This is known as temperature-dependent sex determination, or TDSD, and occurs in other chelonians, notably the green turtle, *Chelonia mydas*.) Temperatures from 75 to 82.5°F (24–28°C) produce only male offspring, but a temperature of 86°F (30°C) gives rise to almost entirely female hatchlings. Because of this sensitivity to temperature global warming may have a significant effect on populations of these and other turtles affected by TDSD in parts of their range.

The young emerge from the nest site between August and October, although hatching takes longer in cooler conditions, and in northern areas they may overwinter underground. When they hatch, the carapace is approximately 1 inch (2.5 cm) long and clearly marked with a central keel and two lateral keels on each side. The young mature quite rapidly and in some cases can breed successfully by the time they are just three years old.

Lifestyle varies significantly depending on distribution. In northern areas the pond turtles hibernate over the winter months, burying themselves in the bottom of the stream or other stretch of water to protect themselves from the cold. Although the water at the surface may freeze, the ice is unlikely to extend down into the muddy bottom. They sometimes bury down as deep as 6 inches (15 cm) to escape being frozen to death.

Around the Mediterranean region, however, European pond turtles often estivate in a similar way during the heat of the summer, when food often becomes scarce.

⬅ *European pond turtles are found in slow-moving or still water with or without vegetation. They feed on fish, invertebrates, amphibians and their larvae, and plants.*

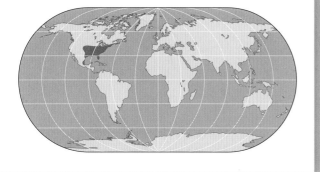

Common name Eastern box turtle

Scientific name *Terrapene carolina*

Family   Emydidae

Suborder Cryptodira

Order   Testudines

Size   Carapace up to 8 in (20 cm) in length

Weight   Approximately 2.2 lb (1 kg)

Key features Carapace relatively domed, usually brownish in color often with variable markings; body predominantly brown with yellow and orange markings particularly on the chin and front legs (depending to some extent on the subspecies and the individual); plastron relatively plain with distinctive hinged flaps front and back, allowing the turtle to seal itself into its shell completely; males generally have reddish irises, but those of females are brownish

Habits   Spends much of its time on land but usually remains close to water; may immerse itself for long periods, especially during dry spells

Breeding Female lays 3–8 eggs in a clutch, sometimes more than once in a season; eggs hatch after 9–18 weeks

Diet   A wide variety of invertebrates as well as smaller vertebrates and carrion; also feeds on vegetable matter and fruit

Habitat   Most likely to be encountered in open areas of woodland; sometimes also occurs in marshy areas

Distribution Eastern United States to northern Mexico

Status   Has declined in various parts of its range

Eastern Box Turtle

Terrapene carolina

Eastern box turtles are among the most well-known turtles and have even appeared on a U.S. postage stamp. Their appearance is variable, and some individuals are thought to live for over 130 years.

THE DOMED CARAPACE of the eastern box turtle is a clue that these turtles spend much of their time on land—more aquatic species have a more streamlined shape. The turtles range widely across eastern parts of the United States from Maine to Florida and south to northern Mexico.

The species is divided into six subspecies that differ in size, markings, and shell shape. The largest race is the Gulf Coast box turtle, *Terrapene carolina major*, which also displays flaring of the hind marginal shields. Its shell is dull in color compared with that of the northern nominate race, *T. c. carolina*. Both these subspecies have four toes on each hind foot. The other two subspecies in the United States are *T. c. triunguis* from Missouri south to Alabama and Texas, and *T. c. bauri* from Florida. Both have three rather than four toes on each of the hind feet. However, *T. c. bauri* can be distinguished by the light pattern of lines radiating across the carapace and two stripes on each side of the head. The carapace of the Mexican races, *T. c. yucatana* and *T. c. mexicana*, is particularly domed—in the latter it is yellow with dark spots.

Hibernation Sites

In northern parts of their range eastern box turtles hibernate in a variety of different places and often use the same site each year. They may prefer to hibernate under water in mud or bury down into soil or under vegetation. Some sites are shared by several box turtles, and they will continue burrowing if the winter proves severe, sometimes digging down distances as great as 24 inches (60 cm). On occasion they

⊕ *Box turtles have two hinges on the plastron, allowing them to close up like a box when threatened. This is the Florida box turtle, Terrapene carolina bauri.*

"Old 1844"

In the past it was something of a tradition for people to carve their initials or dates into the shells of eastern box turtles, particularly in northeastern parts of the United States. Since studies have shown that these turtles are sedentary, researchers have tried to correlate the initials carved on shells of individual turtles with local parish records to come up with a novel way of estimating their age. This led to the discovery of the Hope Valley turtle, also known as "Old 1844," which is believed to be the oldest living vertebrate recorded in the United States.

This particular box turtle had two sets of initials, one of which was E. B. K., and two dates etched on its plastron. It was discovered that in 1844 there was a 19-year-old farmhand called Edward Barber Kenyon working on the land where the turtle was found. The fact that there was no distortion of the carving suggested that the reptile was fully grown then and would therefore have been at least 20 years old at the time. Although it proved impossible to match the second set of initials, G. V. B., alongside the date of July 11, 1860, it was discovered that two families (the Bitgoods and the Bigwoods) had owned the land during that period. It could have been one of their family members who found the turtle again. These two pieces of evidence suggested that Old 1844 was therefore about 138 years old at the date when these enquiries were made.

may also move from one site to another during mild spells, but this can prove fatal if the weather takes an unexpected turn for the worse—the turtles are left stranded and defenseless against the frost.

Those that survive over the winter usually emerge during April, and mating begins

soon after. Their domed shells mean that males have to balance themselves at a semivertical angle when mating. It can be very dangerous for them if they fall over and are unable to right themselves. In most cases, however, they can use their powerful neck to flip their body over if they should fall while mating.

Females lay their eggs typically between May and July, digging the nest site under cover of darkness. The incubation period depends greatly on the temperature and can range from nine weeks to 18 weeks.

⊖ *A closeup of the eastern box turtle shows bright yellow markings on the chin and head. Males have red irises, while those of females are usually brown.*

Common name Spotted turtle

Scientific name *Clemmys guttata*

Family Emydidae

Suborder Cryptodira

Order Testudines

Size Carapace to a maximum of 5 in (13 cm)

Weight Approximately 1.1 lb (0.5 kg)

Key features Carapace relatively low and blackish with an overlying pattern of yellowish spots (which may be more orange in some cases); plastron varies from yellowish to orange in color with variable black blotching; males have brownish chin and eyes; females are more colorful with orange irises and a yellow chin as well as a flatter plastron

Habits Semiaquatic, often wandering on land as well as being found in water

Breeding Female lays a single clutch of 3–8 eggs that hatch after about 10 weeks

Diet Omnivorous; eats especially invertebrates of various types, some of which may be captured on land

Habitat Typically found in marshy areas, sometimes in association with woodland

Distribution North America from the Great Lakes in southern Canada south to northern Florida

Status May be under threat in some areas from habitat disturbance and loss

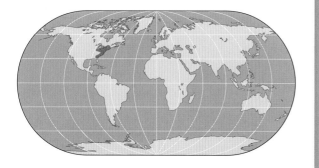

Spotted Turtle *Clemmys guttata*

The best time to see one of the cool-weather spotted turtles is spring—in summer they hide on land waiting for the fall rains before moving back to water, and in winter they hibernate in abandoned muskrat nests.

THE SPOTTED TURTLE is a widely distributed species found in the region of the Great Lakes in southern Canada. Its range extends southward along the Eastern Seaboard of the United States reaching as far as northern Florida, although its distribution becomes more sporadic farther south. Spotted turtles sometimes congregate together in suitable areas. It is not uncommon to see a group basking on a log out of the water; but if disturbed, the turtles will plunge straight back into the water and bury themselves immediately in the mud at the bottom. On land they simply withdraw into their shell if threatened, remaining there until the danger has passed.

Spotted turtles thrive at relatively low temperatures. They may even estivate during the hottest part of the summer, concealing themselves in mud under the water.

These turtles mate quite early in the year, often during March, when the temperature of their surroundings can be just over 43°F (8°C). The female is pursued by one or more males as part of the courtship ritual. The chase can last for up to half an hour, during which time the males may fight among themselves. Mating tends to take place more frequently in the water than on land.

Carefully Constructed Nests

Females usually lay their eggs in June. The female digs a nest in a sunny place, sometimes in quite dry soil. It is not unknown for several different sites to be partially dug and then abandoned before she finds a suitable spot. She uses her hind feet alternately when scooping out the soil. She gives the nest a relatively narrow neck and then widens it

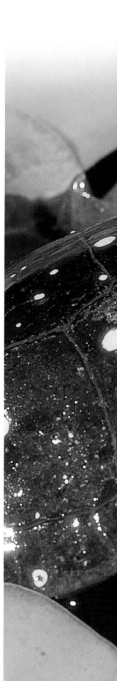

SEE ALSO Turtles 47:8; Freshwater Turtles 47:28

below to create a chamber. Once the nest is completed, the female uses her feet to channel the eggs safely into position. Finally, after a brief pause she fills in the nest using the soil that she dug out previously. She then flattens the surface, using her plastron for this purpose. The whole process lasts for about two hours.

It takes at least 10 weeks before the young hatchlings begin to emerge. In the case of eggs laid in dry ground the young turtles emerge later. In some northern parts of their range the hatchlings may even remain in the ground until the following spring. Young spotted turtles usually have a single yellow spot on each of the

↓ *Spotted turtles are usually found in marshy meadows, bogs, swamps, ponds, or ditches and prefer areas with relatively still water.*

scutes on the carapace apart from the cervical (neck) scute, which is plain. However, a few youngsters may display no markings at all on the carapace, although they have spots on their head and neck.

Hatchlings in general are less heavily spotted than the adults. The extent of spotting also appears to relate to location—one study suggests that individuals from Virginia have smaller, less conspicuous spotting than those occurring farther north. The carapace in hatchlings is about 1.2 inches (3 cm) long, and their slender tail is proportionately longer than that of adults. The plastron is smaller in length relative to the carapace at this stage, but it grows quickly during the first year.

Spotted turtles usually reach sexual maturity at between seven and eight years of age, once they have grown to about 3 inches (8 cm) long. They can live for over half a century. The spots tend to fade in older individuals to the extent that their carapace can appear smooth and black.

Spotted turtles tend to be quite sedentary. They display affinity to their home territory: Studies have shown that they can find their way home from a distance of 0.5 miles (0.8 km).

Spotted turtles spend the winter hibernating either in the mud under water or in a suitable site on land, such as a pile of vegetation. Occasionally a small group can be found together in an abandoned muskrat nest.

Asian Leaf Turtle
Cyclemys dentata

*The generic name of the Asian leaf turtle gives a clue to its appearance—*Cyclemys *means "circle turtle." Hunting by humans for food and the pet trade has caused a decline in some populations in the wild.*

Common name Asian leaf turtle (leaf turtle)

Scientific name *Cyclemys dentata*

Family Emydidae

Suborder Cryptodira

Order Testudines

Size Carapace up to 9.5 in (24 cm); females tend to be larger overall than males

Weight Up to 2.2 lb (1 kg)

Key features Carapace flattened and rounded, light brown through olive to black in color with a keel running down the midline; plastron is light yellowish and narrow compared with carapace; head reddish brown on top and a darker shade of brown on the sides; toes moderately webbed; adults have a hinged plastron

Habits Semiaquatic; moves quite well on land; may climb trees

Breeding Female lays small clutches of 2–3 eggs several times during the year; eggs hatch after about 2–3 months

Diet Omnivorous, eating both plant and animal matter

Habitat Usually found in or near shallow streams

Distribution Found throughout much of Southeast Asia, including Indonesian and Philippine islands

Status Not uncommon in some areas, but the population has probably declined overall; Lower Risk (IUCN)

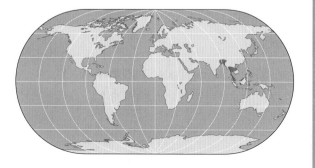

THE COLOR AND FLATTENED SHAPE combined with a pronounced central keel on the carapace of the Asian leaf turtles make them look like dry leaves and help provide camouflage when they are out of water. Adults have a hinge at the front of the plastron, allowing them to seal themselves partially in the shell and giving extra protection.

Asian leaf turtles are quite agile on land. They have only moderately webbed toes, reflecting their semiterrestrial existence, and they are reputed to be able to climb trees on occasion. They are usually found in streams in wooded areas—in Malaysia they are often found in oil palm and rubber plantations. However, in agricultural areas they are vulnerable to the effects of pesticides and other potentially harmful chemicals that can be washed into the waterways.

Very little is documented about their habits in the wild, but they are known to range over a wide area from northern India down across Southeast Asia to various islands, including Java and Sumatra as well as Borneo.

Hunted by Dogs

As with most chelonians occurring in Asia, the leaf turtle has been hunted for food in increasing numbers over recent years. This is thought to have led to local population declines in some parts of its range. Dogs are used to hunt the turtles in Myanmar (formerly Burma), where they are also caught in traditional bamboo traps. In India, however, the leaf turtle is rarely caught. Populations appear quite stable, with large areas of its range within protected areas of hill forest. Any widespread deforestation would, however, represent a threat to those populations.

78 **SEE ALSO** Freshwater Turtles **47:28**

Young Asian leaf turtles are predominantly aquatic at first, but they spend more time on land as they mature. Hatchlings differ in appearance from adults by having a strongly serrated edge to the rear end of the carapace. This may give them some protection against potential predators, since these sharp projections could be a deterrent to snakes and other creatures. In old Asian leaf turtles, however, the central keel on the carapace becomes less pronounced.

New Discoveries

The range of the Asian leaf turtles is wider than previously thought. As recently as 1983 leaf turtles were found in Bangladesh in a stream running through a region of forest in Thainkhali. Discoveries of Asian leaf turtles have since been confirmed in various other parts of Bangladesh, including the Lawachera forest area, Sri Mangal, in Maulvibazar district in the northeast, and in the southeast in the Chunati forest in Chittagong.

Trade in the Vietnamese race of the Asian leaf turtle (which is sometimes divided into two different species known as *Cyclemys tcheponensis* and *C. pulchristriata*) has grown significantly over recent years. Much of it is believed to be illegal, since the turtles are confined to northern and central parts of the country and often occur in protected areas. Its present status is unclear, since really nothing is known about the overall population in Vietnam. In neighboring Laos leaf turtles are believed to have become rarer, but again there is no real information on their past status, which makes any accurate assessment difficult.

Simply finding these particular turtles in the wild is a challenge because of their very effective camouflage. Local hunters are forced to resort to using specially trained dogs, which are at least able to locate them on land. The population in Cambodia is regarded as being significantly larger than in other parts of Southeast Asia, however, and leaf turtles may also be present in China. Here they have been recorded from Yunnan Province and possibly Guangxi; but these reports are based on sightings made in markets rather than in the wild, and they could have originated from elsewhere in the region.

⊕ *Closely related to the Asian leaf turtles is the Vietnamese leaf turtle, Cyclemys (Geoemyda) spengleri. Like the Asian leaf turtles, its carapace has serrated edges, but it has three keels rather than one.*

Tortoises

Tortoises all belong to the family Testudinidae. They live exclusively on land, although they will sometimes wallow in temporary pools of water, usually as a means of cooling themselves. The giants of the group have some of the most restricted distributions of any chelonians, being confined to the Galápagos and Aldabran islands. The greatest diversity of tortoises exists in the African region, where species occur throughout the continent. The family is also represented farther north in Europe as well as in parts of Asia and the New World.

In the genus *Testudo* the Mediterranean spur-thighed tortoise, *T. graeca*, occurs in Europe and Africa. However, Hermann's tortoise, *T. hermanni*, is restricted to the northeastern Mediterranean and adjacent areas of Europe. It lacks the distinctive tubercle on each thigh that is present in *T. graeca* as well as having a longer and more pointed tail.

The biggest of the European species, however, is the marginated tortoise, *T. marginata*, which is found only in southern Greece. It has a distinctive flared appearance to the marginal scutes at the rear of the carapace. The carapace iteself can measure 12 inches (30 cm) long.

African Species

In Africa populations of the Mediterranean spur-thighed tortoise are to be found living under semiarid conditions. They estivate during the hottest months of the year, when food and water are scarce. Farther south on the fringes of the Sahara Desert is the largest of the mainland tortoises, the spurred tortoise, *Geochelone sulcata*, which can reach a maximum carapace length of about 30 inches (76 cm). When weather conditions are bad, it retreats into underground burrows that it digs using its strong legs.

The distribution pattern of the hingeback tortoises that form the genus *Kinixys* reflects the diversity of habitat in which African tortoises can be found—from tropical rain forest to grassland, scrub, and semidesert. Members of the genus include the widely ranging Bell's hingeback, *K. belliana*, which differs very markedly in coloration in different locations—some individuals have plain brown carapaces, while others have very evident patterning on their shells.

The difference in markings is thought to be linked to the type of environment in which the tortoises occur. For example, the eroded hingeback, *K. erosa*, is a species that occurs in tropical forest and can even swim quite well if necessary. It is mahogany-brown in color, which helps conceal its presence on the forest floor. (The patterning of the leopard tortoise, *Geochelone pardalis*, also found in Africa, serves a similar purpose.) The third member of the genus, Home's hingeback, *K. homeana*, has a much more vertical rear to its shell and tends to be a lighter brown color. In common with the other species it is able to seal

---

Common name Tortoises **Family** Testudinidae

Genus *Chersina*—1 species, the South African bowsprit tortoise, *C. angulata*
Genus *Geochelone*—15 species from Asia and the Americas, including the star tortoise, G. elegans; Galápagos giant tortoise, *G. nigra*; spurred tortoise, *G. sulcata*; plowshare tortoise, *G. yniphora*; leopard tortoise, *G. pardalis*
Genus *Gopherus*—4 species from North and Central America, the California gopher tortoise, *G. agassizii*; Texas gopher, *G. berlandieri*; Mexican gopher, *G. flavomarginatus*; Florida gopher, *G. polyphemus*
Genus *Homopus*—4 species from Africa, including the parrot-beaked tortoise, *H. areolatus*, and the speckled Cape tortoise, *H. signatus*
Genus *Kinixys*—3 species of hingeback tortoises from Africa, including Bell's hingeback, *K. belliana*
Genus *Malacochersus*—1 species from Africa, the pancake tortoise, *M. tornieri*
Genus *Psammobates*—3 species from Africa, including the serrated tortoise, *P. oculifera*
Genus *Pyxis*—2 Madagascan species, the Madagascar spider tortoise, *P. arachnoides*, and the Madagascar flat-tailed tortoise, *P. planicauda*
Genus *Testudo*—5 species from Europe, Africa, and Asia, including the Mediterranean spur-thighed tortoise, *T. graeca*; Hermann's tortoise, *T. hermanni*; marginated tortoise, *T. marginata*

 SEE ALSO Turtles 47:8; Tortoise, Leopard 47:92

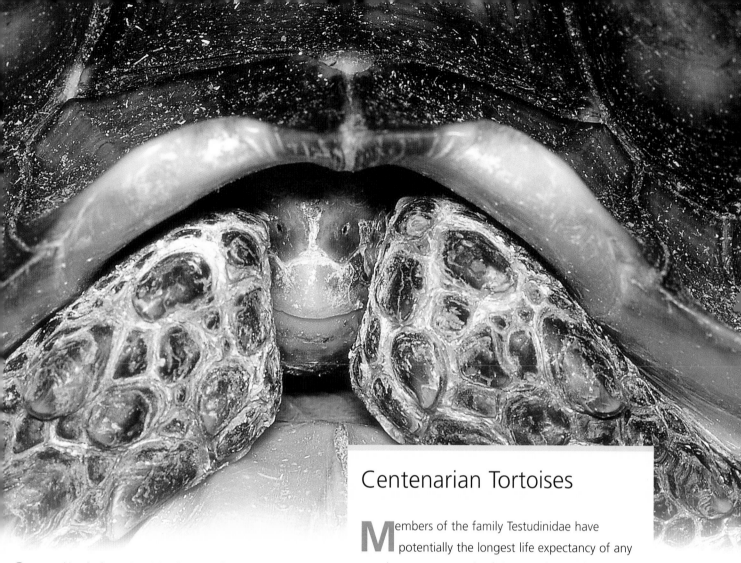

① *Home's hingeback tortoise,* Kinixys homeana *from Africa, hides in its shell. African hingeback tortoises are characterized by a single hinge located about three-quarters of the way along the back of the shell.*

itself in its shell thanks to its hinged plastron. Although it is a forest-dwelling species, it tends to occur in slightly drier areas than the eroded hingeback.

Africa is also home to the world's smallest tortoise, *Homopus signatus*, the speckled Cape tortoise, whose range extends from southern Namibia down to the western Cape. It may only reach a carapace length of 2.4 inches (6 cm) when adult. These tiny tortoises live among rocks, where they can hide away in relative safety. They generally emerge from their retreats only in search of food in the early morning.

Another even more unusual African tortoise found in rocky terrain is *Malacochersus tornieri*, the pancake tortoise, so-called because of its flattened appearance. Occurring in East Africa, this species has sacrificed the rigidity of its shell for the ability to move very quickly and

Centenarian Tortoises

Members of the family Testudinidae have potentially the longest life expectancy of any vertebrates. As a result of the popularity of certain species as pets, it has been possible to discover their potential life span. In the case of the Mediterranean spur-thighed tortoise, *Testudo graeca*, the oldest individual for which reliable information is available lived at Powderham Castle in Devon, England, from 1914 until its death in 2004. It had previously been kept by a family nearby; when it died, this particular tortoise was about 160 years old.

Giant tortoises in the genus *Geochelone* may live even longer, however, as revealed by four individuals that were moved in 1776 from the Seychelles to the nearby island of Mauritius. The last member of the group died after becoming accidentally trapped in a gun emplacement in 1918. Contemporary accounts of its size when it arrived on the island 142 years earlier suggest it was already an adult and so it must have been close to 200 years old when it died.

to retreat from danger under rocks. It uses its body and claws to anchor itself in place, making it very difficult to dislodge from its chosen hiding place.

The islands off eastern Africa are home to various tortoises. However, on Madagascar all four species face a very uncertain future largely because of hunting pressures and habitat disturbance. The status of *Geochelone yniphora*, the plowshare tortoise, notable for the very distinctive prong at the front of its plastron that is used by the male in mating, is especially critical on the island. Wild pigs have proved an additional threat to this species by digging up and destroying its nests. The radiated tortoise, *G. radiata*, with its attractive pattern of light streaks radiating out from a dark background remains more numerous but is considered Vulnerable (IUCN). Its carapace is markedly domed, which emphasizes its patterning. However, young hatchlings have relatively flat shells, albeit still brightly marked.

Asiatic Tortoises

Patterning similar to that of the radiated tortoise is seen in the star tortoise, *Geochelone elegans*, which originates from parts of India, as well as in its Burmese relative, *G. platynota*. Both species are likely to have descended from the same ancestral line as the radiated tortoise. The division probably occurred when the ancient southern continent of Gondawaland split up—India drifted northward and joined with Asia, while the adjacent region of Madagascar remained in the Indian Ocean.

There are seven species of tortoise currently found in Asia, and in general the others are much more subdued

in coloration. An unusual feature of the elongated tortoise, *Geochelone elongata*, however (apart from its relatively long, narrow shell), is the skin in the area around the nostrils, which turns pinkish as the time for nesting approaches. This is caused by increased blood flow to that part of the body, suggesting that the tortoises rely heavily on their ability to detect scents in order to locate a partner. The largest of the Asiatic species is the Burmese brown, *G. emys*, achieving a carapace length of at least 18 inches (46 cm). It too has interesting breeding habits—it is thought that the female remains near the nest to guard the eggs for at least a few days after laying.

Tortoises of the New World

The four species of gopher tortoise in the genus *Gopherus* are restricted to North America, where they inhabit fairly dry terrain. Farther south the Amazon Basin is home to two tropical forest species in the genus *Geochelone* that are similar in appearance to the gophers, leading to the belief that they diverged from a common ancestor about 7 million years ago. The yellow-footed tortoise, *Geochelone denticulata*, is the larger of the two, with a maximum carapace length of 29 inches (74 cm), whereas the more colorful red-footed tortoises, *G. carbonaria*, rarely grow larger than 18 inches (46 cm). Both feed to a significant degree on fruit as well as greenstuff. Interestingly, in spite of their close relationship and the fact that their distribution overlaps in some parts of their range, they do not interbreed. They avoid this by recognizing specific courtship movements made by the males, which differ in each species. Clues relating to smell may also be used.

The most southerly representative of the tortoises in the New World is the Chaco tortoise, *Geochelone chilensis*, which lives in grassland areas in Chile and Argentina. It occurs quite close to the tip of South America, but it avoids extreme temperatures by retreating to underground burrows during cold or dry periods.

The Harshest Environment

Horsfield's tortoise, *Testudo horsfieldii*, has the most northerly distribution of any tortoise—the plains of Kazakhstan, part of the former USSR. The tortoises emerge from hibernation in spring and are active for only about three months before retreating to their underground burrows by July. This is a reflection of the harsh climate in which they occur, where the winters are very cold and the summers are hot and dry. Suitable vegetation is only available during this short spring period. They must also use this time to mate and, in the case of females, lay their eggs before returning to their burrows.

Land Tortoises in Australia

There are no land tortoises occurring in Australia today, but in the past there used to be a population of bizarre horned tortoises, known by their family name of meiolaniids. Their appearance was quite unlike that of chelonians that we would recognize today. These unusual tortoises were characterized by a pair of hornlike projections on their head. The "horns" could be spaced up to 24 inches (60 cm) apart. It is thought that, together with hard plates that were present on the upper surface of the tail,

they helped provide these large tortoises with "armor" to protect them against would-be predators.

The ancestors of this group arose during the Cretaceous Period around 100 million years ago in the region that is now South America. Later they reached Australia, occurring on the southeast of the continent and also on nearby islands, notably Lord Howe Island off the coast of New South Wales in eastern Australia, where they survived until as recently as 120,000 years ago. They appear to have died out in South America much earlier, however, around 70 million years ago.

The way in which the meiolaniids arrived in Australia from South America has been a source of puzzlement, although members of the family Chelidae (snake-necked turtles) are still found on both continents today. It is believed that the ancestors of both families were actually present in Antarctica (which served as a land bridge to connect these continents) at a time when it lay much closer to the equator and was therefore significantly warmer. The discovery of the fossilized remains of chelonians in Antarctica dating back to the Miocene Epoch about 20 million years ago appears to confirm this theory.

Galápagos Giant Tortoise

Geochelone nigra

Common name Galápagos giant tortoise

Scientific name *Geochelone nigra*

Family   Testudinidae

Suborder   Cryptodira

Order   Testudines

Size   Carapace from 29 in (74 cm) to over 4 ft (1.2 m) in length depending on subspecies

Weight   Approximately 500 lb (227 kg)

Key features Large, bulky tortoise; shell shape varies depending on subspecies; neck often long; carapace and plastron are a uniform dull shade of brown; males have longer, thicker tails than females and often have a more yellowish area on the lower jaw and throat

Habits   Seeks out sun in the morning, basking before setting off to feed; usually inactive in the latter part of the afternoon, sometimes wallowing in a muddy hollow; quite agile despite its large size

Breeding   Female lays clutch of 2–10 eggs, occasionally up to 16; eggs hatch usually after 3–4 months

Diet   A wide range of vegetation and fruit; can even eat the spiny shoots of the prickly pear cactus

Habitat   Generally prefers upland areas

Distribution Restricted to the Galápagos Islands

Status   Endangered, critically in some cases (IUCN)

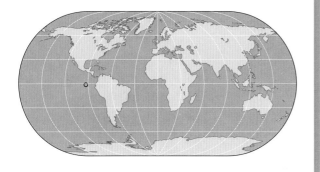

The giant tortoises of the Galápagos Islands have played an important part in the field of biological science. They provided one of the pieces of evidence used by Charles Darwin to support his theory of evolution, which stunned the world in the 19th century.

THE BRITISH NATURALIST AND EXPLORER Charles Darwin visited the Galápagos Islands as the zoologist aboard *H.M.S. Beagle* in 1835. The population of giant tortoises, *Geochelone nigra*, on these volcanic islands had already been known to European whaling ships for many years. Crews regularly used to take the giant tortoises on board, and the creatures were able to survive for up to 14 months without food before being butchered and eaten.

Ships' Mutton

The numbers removed are quite staggering. Ships' logs reveal that a total of 115,000 were taken off the islands between 1811 and 1844, and the trade was well established by the time Darwin visited. The meat of the tortoises was even named "Galápagos mutton." They were not just used for food, however—their fat was distilled into oil along with their eggs. This plundering had a damaging effect on the tortoise populations, not all of which survived.

It is thought that there were 14 distinct races, or subspecies, on the islands. Only 11 are still there today—one of them, *Geochelone nigra abingdoni,* is facing imminent extinction and has been reduced to a single individual.

After such heavy persecution it is remarkable that it was not until 1876 that the first of these tortoises died out. It used to live on Charles Island and was flat backed with a very shiny shell. The next to disappear was the undescribed Barrington Island race, which was certainly extinct by 1890. Subsequently,

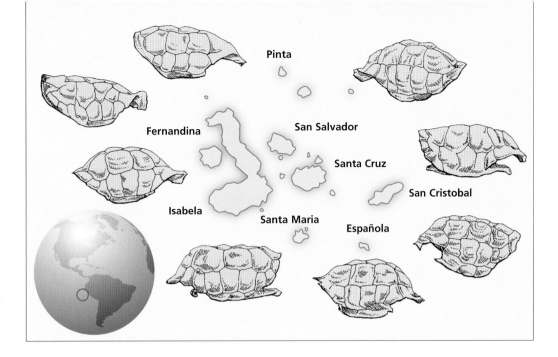

the Narborough Island tortoise with its
characteristically flared marginal shields located
at the back of the carapace had also
disappeared by 1906.

Where Did They Come From?

The Galápagos Islands themselves
consist of a group of 20 islands
located approximately 600 miles
(1,000 km) off the coast of Ecuador
in northern South America. They are
volcanic in origin, which
means that there was no
indigenous wildlife on
the islands.

It is thought that the
ancestors of the giant
tortoises drifted south
from Central America
through the Pacific Ocean
and were ultimately
washed up on the
beaches. They managed
to colonize and spread

⊝ The Galápagos giant
tortoise is the largest and
heaviest living tortoise. This
old male roams across the
landscape at a speed of just
0.16 miles per hour (0.3 km/h).

Lonesome George

The population of giant tortoises on Abingdon Island, *Geochelone nigra abingdoni*, was particularly vulnerable to trade in tortoise meat in the 18th and 19th centuries because of its location—it was the first island in the archipelago to be encountered by whalers heading down toward Antarctic waters. Surprisingly, the population just managed to survive this era until the introduction of three goats in 1958. They stripped the tortoises' habitat, and by 1971 there was thought to be only one surviving male on the island. Named "Lonesome George" by staff at the Charles Darwin Scientific Research Station on Santa Cruz Island where he now resides, this individual is estimated to be between 50 and 80 years old.

Sadly, in spite of intensive searching on Abingdon Island for more than 30 years, it has proven impossible to find George a mate, and he shows no interest in breeding with females of any other subspecies. He is likely to be the last of his line, although he is only middle-aged at present. With a potential life expectancy approaching 200 years, there is the possibility that some of today's oldest tortoises on the islands were already resident there as hatchlings at the time of Charles Darwin's visit in 1835.

across the islands, or (more probably) there were several such strandings. Recent studies involving mitochondrial DNA, which is used for tracking ancestries, have revealed that the oldest group of tortoises can be found on Española. A second wave of colonization established populations on southern Isabela, Volcan Darwin, and Volcan Alcedo, followed by a third on other islands within the group.

It may seem unlikely that tortoises could drift through the ocean and end up being washed onto such tiny specks of land. Yet they are not the only reptilian colonists from the American mainland on these islands. Marine iguanas, *Amblyrhynchus cristatus*, thought to be descended from the green iguana, *Iguana iguana*, also live there. It is not uncommon even today for tortoises to be carried out to sea on floodwaters—they are, in fact, well equipped to

survive in these surroundings, remaining afloat with little effort and bobbing along on the waves. They do not need to eat, since their body stores fat that can be metabolized. It is possible that the early reptiles made the crossing not in the sea itself but by floating on debris, a process known as rafting.

What is particularly significant is that there would not necessarily have been any need for more than one tortoise to have reached the Galápagos Islands in the first instance to begin the colonization process. A mature female that had bred previously would not have needed to mate again in these new surroundings in order to lay fertile eggs, since she could still have

⊕ *As night falls over the Alcedo Volcano on Isabela Island, a group of giant tortoises wallow in a pool to cool down and gain relief from ticks and mosquitoes.*

been carrying viable sperm in her reproductive tract. Based on studies of modern chelonians, we know that a female may well be able to lay regularly for as long as four years without a male, producing many tens of offspring during this period. The young would have hatched in a relatively safe environment, so the population probably started to increase in number quite rapidly.

It is impossible to calculate how many of these island giants there were, but some people suggest there could have been hundreds of thousands of them at one stage. The biggest problem they would have faced would have been the ability to find enough food in a limited range. As a result, they evolved physical adaptations to reflect their environment, a fact that excited Darwin during his visit.

⊕ *Food and water can be scarce. The Galápagos giant tortoise eats prickly pear cacti and fruits, bromeliads, water ferns, leaves, and grass. It can store large amounts of water, enabling it to survive the long dry season.*

Three Types of Tortoise

Zoologists now tend to classify the different races of Galápagos giant tortoises in three separate categories based on these physical adaptations. First, there are those known as saddlebacks, a reference to the way in which the shell at the front of the carapace is raised above the neck. These individuals tend to be found on islands where conditions are relatively arid. This adaptation enables them to browse on taller plants that are less affected by periods of drought than vegetation growing at ground level. Their neck is long as well, and their limbs are elongated, so they can use their height to maximum effect.

Remarkably, the plants on the islands have responded to the browsing behavior of the tortoises. Where saddleback populations occurred—for example, on Abingdon Island— the prickly pear cactus, *Opuntia*, which is one of the tortoise's main foods, altered its shape too. It developed a tougher outer casing and adopted a more treelike growth pattern, making it harder for the tortoises to feed on it.

On islands where saddlebacks are not present, the prickly pear's shape is unaffected.

Second, there are Galápagos giant tortoises with a more typically dome-shaped appearance and a short neck. They tend to be encountered on upland areas of the islands where grazing conditions are generally good. The third group consists of tortoises that display intermediate characteristics between these two extremes.

The legacy of the seafarers' visits to the islands is still apparent today and represents an ongoing threat to the survival of various populations, in spite of the fact that hunting has ceased and the tortoises are fully protected. Today's problems revolve largely around the other creatures that were brought on the ships and were frequently abandoned on the islands. They too have thrived, often to the detriment of the tortoises. In order to supplement their rations, sailors often left goats on remote outposts, quite oblivious to the environmental problems they would cause. On the Galápagos Islands goats have competed with the tortoises for food and can destroy their nests as well. Pigs are also a hazard, since they will actively seek out nests using their keen sense of smell.

Saving the Tortoises

A number of different programs are being undertaken to conserve and increase the populations of giant tortoises, not least by controlling the introduction of mammals,

including black rats, which are another legacy of sailing ships that visited the islands. Intensive captive-breeding programs are also underway both in the Galápagos and abroad. Zoological collections around the world are cooperating for this purpose.

The success achieved can be remarkable, as shown by the work of the Darwin Foundation, which has hatched over 2,500 young tortoises in barely 40 years. This has provided a major boost to a population estimated at no more than 10,000 individuals in total. The tortoises are kept safely in pens until they are three years old and large enough to be no longer at risk of predation by endemic birds of prey. It may take a quarter of a century for these tortoises to become sexually mature.

Even today, however, unexpected hazards can occur and threaten populations of the tortoises, as in October 1998, when lava from the erupting Cerro Azul volcano started to flow toward a group of tortoises. An airlift was organized, but in spite of these efforts, a small number of tortoises died from being trapped in the lava or the resulting fires nearby. They included a member of the critically endangered subspecies *G. n. guntheri,* whose total population is at most about 100 individuals. Shifting the gigantic tortoises is a difficult and costly exercise. Helicopters were used to ferry them to the coast from 5 miles (8 km) or so inland, from where they could be taken in boats to the safety of the breeding center.

Reproduction

Male Galápagos giant tortoises often make a roaring sound when mating. Courtship itself is a fairly brutal process, with the larger males battering at the shells

⊙ *The sailors have gone, but today tourists still flock to see the wildlife on the islands, including the giant tortoises on Santa Cruz.*

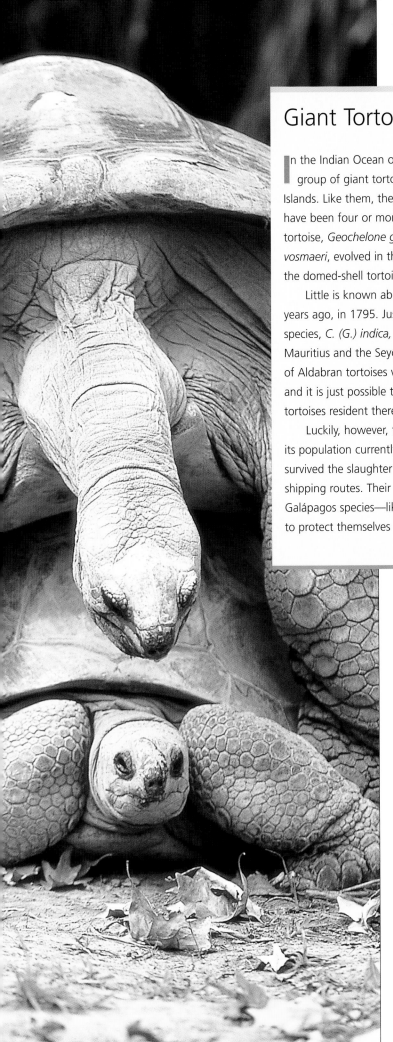

Giant Tortoises Elsewhere

In the Indian Ocean off the southeast coast of Africa a completely separate group of giant tortoises suffered a fate similar to those on the Galápagos Islands. Like them, they were captured in large numbers by mariners. There may have been four or more species, of which only one survives today—the Aldabran tortoise, *Geochelone gigantea*. Interestingly, a saddleback form, *Cylindraspis (G.) vosmaeri*, evolved in the region—on the island of Rodriguez—and was larger than the domed-shell tortoises, *C. (G.) peltastes*, which were also found there.

Little is known about these two species, which became extinct about 200 years ago, in 1795. Just prior to this the last surviving example of the Reunion species, *C. (G.) indica,* had died out as well. Native populations also existed on Mauritius and the Seychelles, but information about them is sketchy. A number of Aldabran tortoises were taken to the Seychelles and Mauritius in the 1800s, and it is just possible that they might have interbred with any surviving native tortoises resident there.

Luckily, however, the future of the Aldabran species itself seems secure, with its population currently consisting of over 100,000 individuals. Its ancestors survived the slaughter essentially because of their remote location away from shipping routes. Their behavior is similar in some respects to that of the Galápagos species—like them, they wallow in mud to cool their bodies and to protect themselves against mosquito bites.

⊖ *Mating in large reptiles can be a dangerous business. This is a mating pair of captive Aldabran tortoises,* Geochelone gigantea, *in the Seychelles.*

of the females and pinning them down by clambering on top.

Females lay their eggs between July and December, but this varies on different islands. Although clutches contain relatively few eggs— usually from just two to 10 but occasionally up to 16—females may lay more than once during this period. The eggs themselves have hard shells and are spherical in shape. The incubation period lasts on average between three and four months but can extend up to seven months. The young tortoises emerge during the wet season when there is fresh grass and other vegetation available for them to eat. The carapace of a newly hatched individual measures about 2.4 inches (6 cm) in length.

Gopher tortoise
(*Gopherus polyphemus*)

Common/scientific names Desert gopher, *Gopherus agassizii;* gopher tortoise, *G. polyphemus;* Berlandier's gopher, *G. berlandieri;* Bolson tortoise, *G. flavomarginatus*

Family	Testudinidae
Suborder	Cryptodira
Order	Testudines
Size	Carapace length from 9 in (23 cm) in *G. berlandieri* to 20 in (50 cm) in *G. agassizii*
Weight	Approximately 8 lb (3.6 kg) to 15 lb (6.8 kg)
Key features	Carapace domed; front limbs flattened for burrowing and bear thick hard scales; hind feet stumpy and elephantine; all feet lack webbing; plastron in males is concave; carapace generally some shade of brown or tan but variable according to species; plastron usually yellowish
Habits	Strictly terrestrial; retreat into burrows to avoid excessive temperatures; desert gophers and Bolson tortoises may hibernate
Breeding	Most mate in spring, and females may nest 2 or 3 times a season; all are egg layers, with clutch sizes ranging from 2–15 eggs that hatch in late summer or fall
Diet	Herbivores; diet includes plants, fruits, and grasses
Habitat	Prefer sandy soil; varies from arid desert to scrub woodlands, grasslands, and forests
Distribution	Southern United States south to Mexico
Status	Numbers in decline due to habitat change and land development; *G. polypheumus, G. flavomarginatus,* and *G. agassizii* are Vulnerable (IUCN); all species listed on CITES Appendix I or II

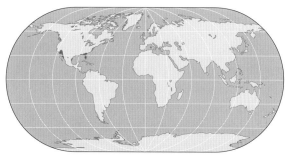

Gopher Tortoises *Gopherus* sp.

The gopher tortoises are the only remaining land tortoises found in North America today. Sadly, all four species are declining in number and need to be protected.

GOPHER TORTOISES ARE MORE DEPENDENT on their underground burrows than other tortoises and most of them dig much longer tunnels. They are not social by nature, however, and do not share their burrows with their own kind.

There are four species in the genus *Gopherus*. First, the desert gopher, *G. agassizii*, ranges from northern California down to parts of Mexico including Baja California and Sonora. It is well equipped for tunneling thanks to its powerful front legs. It is the largest species, reaching a maximum carapace length of about 20 inches (50 cm). Many invertebrates invade its tunnels, and they in turn attract predatory species such as the gopher frog, *Rana capito*, various rodents, and rattlesnakes, *Crotalus* species. However, they all seem to coexist quite peacefully with the tortoise. These gophers emerge to feed on vegetation such as cacti in the arid areas where they occur.

The second species, the gopher tortoise, *G. polyphemus*, occurs from South Carolina through Florida south to Louisiana. It is quite small with a carapace of up to 12 inches (30 cm) long. Females lay their eggs from April to June. Unfortunately, studies have shown that nest predation by mammals, including armadillos, *Dasypus novemcinctus*, and striped skunks, *Mephitis mephitis*, can be high. Estimates suggest that fewer than 6 percent of eggs laid give rise to young tortoises that survive their first year. They are about 20 years old before they can breed for the first time.

Third, Berlandier's gopher, *G. berlandieri,* is found in more western areas from southern

⊕ *The gopher tortoise,* Gopher polyphemus, *digs its burrows in well-drained, sandy soil in places such as sandhill oak forests, pine flatwoods, oak hammocks, and beach scrub forests.*

 SEE ALSO Tortoises **47**:80; Vipers and Pit Vipers **50**:50

Texas across the Mexican border. (It is also known as the Texas desert tortoise.) It is the smallest member of the genus with a maximum carapace length of about 9 inches (23 cm). Unlike its bigger relatives, it does not dig tunnels itself—it prefers to invade those dug by other animals. If necessary, however, it will excavate a simple retreat in the ground using the gular prong at the front of the plastron. The hollow is usually well concealed in vegetation.

The fourth member of the genus is the Bolson tortoise, *G. flavomarginatus*. It occurs in Mexico in a limited area approximately 75 miles (121 km) long between Chihuahua, Coahuila, and Durango. It is well equipped to dig, and its tunnels can be over 33 feet (10 m) long. In the past this species used to extend as far north as Oklahoma; but its range has contracted dramatically, and it is now considered to be highly endangered.

Burrowing Experts

In normal circumstances young gophers start to create their burrows soon after hatching and may remain there throughout their potentially long lives, digging at intervals. The tunnel is not just a refuge to escape the worst of the desert sun; it also helps provide the tortoises with a more humid environment below ground. When they emerge, they follow paths that can be clearly made out by the pattern of flat, shortened vegetation where they have been grazing. Gophers benefit from water present in the plants and fruits that they eat, so they do not need to drink regularly, although they may drink condensation in their burrows.

A Health Concern

Unfortunately, there are serious risks involved in moving populations of gopher tortoises for conservation purposes, including the endangered Bolson tortoise, *G. flavomarginatus*. The dry environment in which the gophers occur may be one reason why they appear extremely vulnerable to mycoplasmosis, which often results in a fatal infection of the upper respiratory tract. Some tortoises can be carriers of the mycoplasma microbes that cause this illness, so that they represent an unseen hazard to other individuals with which they come into contact.

Leopard Tortoise

Geochelone pardalis

A large and attractively marked tortoise with a distinctive pattern and relatively high-domed shell, the leopard tortoise is widely distributed across sub-Saharan Africa.

Common name Leopard tortoise

Scientific name *Geochelone pardalis*

Family Testudinidae

Suborder Cryptodira

Order Testudines

Size Carapace to a maximum of 24 in (60 cm)

Weight Up to 70 lb (32 kg)

Key features Carapace domed and attractive with a variable pattern of dark markings on a light yellowish-horn background; skin is relatively light in color, but some individuals are darker overall than others; male has a longer tail than female, and its plastron is slightly concave; young hatchlings have egg tooth on snout

Habits Wanders through grassland and savanna; diurnal

Breeding Female lays individual clutches ranging from 5–30 eggs; eggs hatch after 8–18 months

Diet Eats virtually all plant matter, including dry grass when other food is in short supply

Habitat Open areas of country

Distribution Eastern and southern parts of Africa from Ethiopia south to the Cape

Status Relatively common but at risk from being hunted for food

THE MARKINGS OF LEOPARD TORTOISES are surprisingly individual. Their coloration differs in some parts of their range, helping them blend in with the background of the particular locality. Their common name comes from the patterning on the carapace, which is similar to that of a leopard's spots.

Leopard tortoises rank among the most prolific of all species of tortoise in terms of breeding frequency. Females lay up to six clutches in succession with intervals of just a few weeks in between. Courtship is a violent encounter, however: The male simply rams the shell of his intended mate.

Males can be identified by having a longer tail and a slight concavity on the plastron, which helps facilitate mating. It is not uncommon for them to utter a wheezing, grunting sound with their mouth held open when they are on the female's back.

Underground Nursery

Each clutch of eggs is buried in a separate nest up to 12 inches (30 cm) below the surface. It can take a considerable period of time for the young tortoises to hatch, and they may spend as long as a year or more underground according to some reports. As in the case of other chelonians, they cut their way out of the shell. They use the temporary egg tooth that is present on their snout for this purpose and dig up to the surface.

Their carapace measures about 2 inches (5 cm) at this stage, and the hatchlings can weigh up to 1.75 ounces (50 g) each. They are likely to reach about 2.2 pounds (1 kg) by the

⊕ A newly hatched leopard tortoise emerges from its burrow in Transvaal, South Africa. Its highly patterned shell will act as a form of camouflage in open areas.

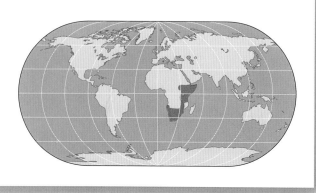

time they are eight years old, and they subsequently grow more quickly, doubling their weight every two years if food is plentiful. Both sexes are then able to breed by the time they are approximately 15 years of age.

A number of creatures prey on young leopard tortoises, ranging from birds such as large hornbills to various mammals. Grassland fires can represent a hazard too. Often, however, the tortoises retreat inside their shell, and the flames move over them very quickly, leaving them unharmed. They are more likely to die as the result of a fall, which can cause serious cracks to their shells.

Few animals disturb adult leopard tortoises, but they are hunted for their meat in various parts of their range. Their shells may subsequently be used to make musical instruments. As they grow

Homing Ability

Aside from laying sequential clutches of eggs at short intervals, these tortoises display another characteristic most commonly associated with marine turtles—they have a strong homing instinct. This was confirmed when a group of leopard tortoises were moved a distance of some 8 miles (13 km) from their regular home range. They subsequently returned within a period of two weeks. They even managed to scale a wire mesh fence that stood 4 feet (1.2 m) high. How these tortoises navigated their way back to familiar territory is unclear, but they may have relied on the earth's magnetic field at first. Then as they got closer to home, familiar landmarks such as trees may have provided guidance, since tortoises have excellent vision. There is an advantage for creatures such as tortoises in staying in a particular area—they will learn where food and, possibly more significantly, a supply of drinking water are likely to be found.

older, the bright coloration tends to disappear, and their shell becomes grayish in color. Individual leopard tortoises are likely to live for over 50 years.

Subspecies

The appearance of the leopard tortoise can vary throughout its range, but only two distinct subspecies have been identified. The most widespread is *G. p. babcocki*, which extends from the Sudan to southeastern and eastern parts of Africa. In contrast, the nominate subspecies, *G. p. pardalis*, is confined to the southwestern corner of Africa, where its population has declined over recent years. Its carapace is not as tall overall, and it has a flat rather than a domed top to its shell.

CROCODILIANS

The ancestry of today's crocodiles stretches back over 265 million years, making them one of the oldest vertebrate groups on the planet. In common with the turtles they survived the major upheaval that resulted in the disappearance of the dinosaurs about 65 million years ago. By that time the direct ancestors of today's crocodilians had already developed.

Some of the early crocodiles are believed to have been much larger than those existing now. Remains of *Deinosuchus* have been unearthed in various parts of the United States. Its skull measured over 6.5 feet (2 m). Based on the head to body ratios of modern crocodilians, it could easily have grown to over 50 feet (15.2 m) long and may have weighed as much as 6 tons (6,096 kg). These crocodilians probably preyed on duck-billed dinosaurs, since fossilized remains of both species have been found together.

Even the direct ancestors of today's species are known to have been larger in the past, as shown by the fossilized remains of caimans. The largest-known example yet unearthed is *Caiman neivensis*, which occurred in the area of present-day Colombia and grew up to 30 feet (9.1 m) in length, dwarfing modern species. While the majority of crocodilians today inhabit fresh water, there were many crocodilians in the past that roamed the world's oceans and were fearsome predators in the sea. Today just

two species are regularly encountered in the marine environment: The saltwater crocodile, *Crocodylus porosus*, occurs in the Indo-Pacific region, and the American crocodile, *Crocodylus acutus,* in the Caribbean region. A number of others, including the Nile crocodile, *C. niloticus*, the American alligator, *Alligator mississippiensis*, and the common caiman, *Caiman crocodilus*, can be found in the sea occasionally.

Crocodiles that live in marine habitats face the inevitable challenge of avoiding the risk of dehydration, which could be fatal. Their thick skin helps prevent loss of water by osmosis, however, and there are also highly effective salt glands located at the back of the mouth that excrete sodium chloride from the body. They are present in all crocodiles, not just those that range out to sea, which suggests that their ancestors originated from the marine environment.

Some crocodilians in the past appear to have been primarily terrestrial. It is assumed that they died out

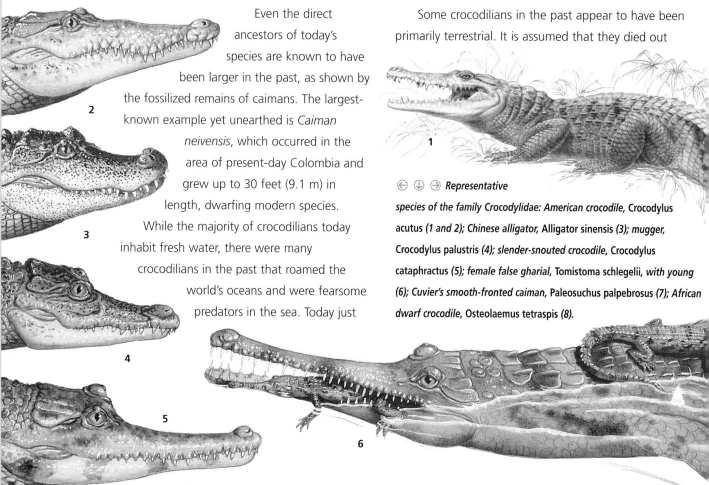

← ↓ → *Representative species of the family Crocodylidae: American crocodile, Crocodylus acutus (1 and 2); Chinese alligator, Alligator sinensis (3); mugger, Crocodylus palustris (4); slender-snouted crocodile, Crocodylus cataphractus (5); female false gharial, Tomistoma schlegelii, with young (6); Cuvier's smooth-fronted caiman, Paleosuchus palpebrosus (7); African dwarf crocodile, Osteolaemus tetraspis (8).*

largely because they were no match for the mammalian hunters that colonized the land after the end of the Cretaceous Period about 65 million years ago. The New Caledonia crocodile, *Quinkana fortirostrum*, was the last survivor of this group, evolving at a stage before the island for which it is named separated from the much larger landmass of Australia. Growing to approximately 6.5 feet (2 m), these crocodiles had powerful limb muscles to help them move on land. They lived right through until the first native people reached the islands about 2,000 years ago, but they had disappeared before the arrival of the Europeans.

In the past crocodilians also had a much wider distribution than they do today, and remains have even been unearthed in Europe. Although there are no surviving representatives of the family there today, they are found on all other continents. The basic appearance of crocodilians has changed relatively little over a long period of time—recognizable ancestors of the American alligator existed for over 5 million years in the same area of the United States where the species is still found.

Predatory Lifestyles

The appearance of the snout of a crocodilian gives a clear indication of its feeding habits. Those with long, narrow jaws with relatively small, sharp teeth such as Johnston's crocodile, *C. johnstoni* from Australia, are primarily fish-eaters. Others with broader jaws, for example, the saltwater crocodile, *C. porosus* (also from Australia), prey predominantly on mammals. In some cases they can catch creatures that are almost as large as themselves.

The fearsome teeth in the jaws of crocodiles are regularly replaced throughout their lives, although the

7

8

rate of replacement slows down with age. It is actually the difference in the arrangement of the teeth that distinguishes alligators from crocodiles. In alligators the lower set of teeth is concealed when the mouth is closed, whereas in true crocodiles the fourth tooth in the lower jaw remains visible when the jaws are closed, sliding into a notch rather than being concealed in a pit.

The tremendous power in the jaws of large crocodilians is used to deadly effect to seize and incapacitate mammalian prey, dragging the victim under water. Crocodiles usually kill their prey by drowning. The crushing force that can be inflicted by the jaws of a large crocodile is equivalent to about 11 tons (13 tonnes). Yet, remarkably, the muscles that open the jaws are very weak. A simple rubber band applied around the jaws of a young crocodile less than 6.5 feet (2 m) in length will be enough to keep it from moving these muscles.

Their teeth are not equipped to chew food, so it is not uncommon for crocodiles to work together to dismantle a carcass. One individual holds onto the body while the other tears off a chunk, usually by spinning around under water. The crocodiles then raise their head and proceed to gulp the whole piece of food down into their gullet.

Many large crocodilians rely on their ability to ambush prey as their main hunting strategy, lurking close to the water's edge where mammals and birds come to drink. The design of the crocodile's body is ideally suited to this type of hunting, since it can rest with just the top of the ears and eyes positioned out of the water. It can also raise the nostrils located on the tip of the snout above the water in order to breathe. Since they have no lips, however, water flows into the crocodilian's mouth when it is submerged. A special flap at the back of the mouth stops the crocodile from swallowing the water.

Crocodilians occur in a wide range of habitats. Some favor marshland areas, while others are restricted to rivers. The small African dwarf crocodile, *Osteolaemus tetraspis*, lives in forested areas, where it inhabits small waterways. As its name suggests, it is the smallest of all contemporary crocodiles, reaching a maximum length of approximately 6.5 feet (2 m).

⊕ *Caimans are distinguished by having broad, blunt snouts, and the teeth in the lower jaw lie inside the mouth when closed. This broad-nosed caiman,* Caiman latirostris, *is feeding on a catfish in Argentina.*

Reproduction

All crocodilians reproduce by means of eggs. Since males grow at a faster rate than females, they mature earlier, usually at about seven years old, by which stage they have reached a length of about 6 feet (1.8 m). Females are unlikely to lay for the first time until they are about nine years of age. While most crocodilians construct an elaborate nest mound, the American crocodile, *C. acutus*, is unusual—females often simply bury their eggs in a hole dug in the sand. In many cases the female guards the nest throughout the incubation period, occasionally with assistance from the male, and helps the young into the

water once they emerge. Just as in the case of many chelonians (turtles and tortoises), the incubation temperature determines the sex of the offspring. The actual temperature parameters vary significantly, however, among different species.

Crocodilian Senses

Since crocodilians tend to hunt at night, their eyes have typical vertical, slit-shaped pupils that maximize the amount of light entering them. They also have a reflective layer called the *tapetum lucidum* at the back of the retina. It acts like a mirror, reflecting back the available light and helping provide a clearer image. As a result, censuses of crocodiles in an area are usually carried out at night by flashlight, because this causes their eyes to glow in the dark and makes counting them straightforward.

However, this technique has the disadvantage that it gives little indication of an individual's size.

Crocodiles can also see well during the daytime, and they have color vision to help them. They also have a protective transparent shield, known as the nictitating membrane, that covers the eyes under water without impairing their vision.

If the water is muddy, crocodiles can use their keen sense of smell. They also have very acute hearing, which not only helps them hunt but is also important for communication. For example, a female is able to detect her young calling from within the nest once they are ready to hatch. Adult crocodiles keep in touch with each other by bellowing and by slapping their head down on the water's surface. This noise carries some distance, so it can be detected by other crocodiles in the area.

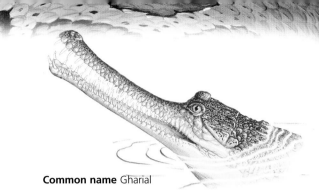

Common name Gharial

Scientific name *Gavialis gangeticus*

Subfamily Gavialinae

Family Crocodylidae

Order Crocodylia

Size Up to 21 feet (6.4 m) overall

Weight Large males may weigh up to 1 ton (1,016 kg)

Key features Body relatively slim with an elongated, narrow snout; in males snout has a knob at its tip; teeth narrow, sharp, and interlocking; color usually olive-green with dark bands across the body; rear feet heavily webbed

Habits Highly aquatic

Breeding Female lays clutch of 28–43 eggs; eggs hatch after 65 or 80 days

Diet Predominantly fish; older individuals may also catch birds; reputedly scavenges on the cremated remains of humans

Habitat Rivers

Distribution Northern parts of the Indian subcontinent

Status Endangered (IUCN); listed on CITES Appendix I

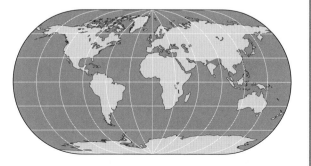

Gharial

Gavialis gangeticus

Known since ancient times, the gharial is the only living species of the subfamily Gavialinae. It is highly aquatic and well adapted for life in the deep waters of the great rivers of the Indian subcontinent.

THE UNUSUAL NAME of these distinctive crocodilians comes from the Indian word *ghara*. It describes the swollen handle on a type of cooking pot popular in the north of the country, which is said to be the same shape as the snout of a mature male gharial.

The gharial's range has contracted significantly over recent years. It is the last in the lineage of a much larger group that first emerged in the fossil record about 20 million years ago. These early gharials ranged across the Americas as well as in Africa and Asia.

Today's species is also much smaller in size than its ancestors. They could grow to at least 56 feet (17 m) long. Nevertheless, present-day gharials can reach 21 feet (6.4 m) long from the snout to the tip of the tail. Despite their size, they pose no threat to people. They are adept hunters, however, and can seize even quite large fish using the sharp teeth in their narrow jaws. They then raise their head out of the water and deftly reposition the fish as necessary, making it easy to swallow. Waterbirds may occasionally be caught as well.

Threatened Species

Over the course of the past century gharials have faced a number of threats to their survival. They used to be heavily hunted for sport. Then they began to be killed for their skins, which were used in the manufacture of leather goods. More recently, the growth in human populations has also contributed to the gharial's decline. The swollen snout of the males has acquired an ill-founded reputation as an aphrodisiac. As a result, they have been heavily hunted compared with females, creating a serious imbalance in the surviving population.

⊕ *The gharial's needlelike teeth are ideal for seizing slippery fish. Lying submerged, it snatches fish as they go by, but it has to raise its snout above the surface when swallowing to avoid taking in too much water.*

Gharial eggs, which are the largest eggs laid by any crocodilian and weigh about 5.6 oz (160 g), are also considered to be a rare delicacy. Nests may be dug up and destroyed for this reason.

Changes in habitat, such as the construction of a dam at Kalagarh on the Ramganga River, have also had a serious effect on the numbers of these crocodilians. Gharials prefer fast-flowing rivers, but the blocking of the river flow by the dam caused flooding over a wide area and effectively destroyed their breeding habitat.

Ranching (which involves taking eggs from nests in the wild and hatching them in incubators) and captive-breeding programs are both being used by Indian zoologists to increase gharial numbers. Their efforts have been relatively successful, with the gharial population increasing from a low point of about 250 individuals in 1974 to as many as 2,500 by 2004. One of the major release sites for the young gharials is the National Chambal Sanctuary, where there is plenty of suitable habitat in which they can safely increase in numbers. The river system in this area extends

The Misjudged Gharial

Gharials were persecuted because they fed on fish; any of these crocodilians that had the misfortune to become entangled in fishermen's nets were likely to be killed as a consequence. Ironically, however, as the number of gharials fell, so did fish stocks. This apparent discrepancy was resolved once it became clear that gharials actually preferred to prey on fish that were themselves predatory by nature; by keeping their numbers in check, the gharials ensured that there were more fish for local people to catch.

Gharials also suffered persecution because it was not uncommon for individuals to be found with bracelets and other similar items of jewelry in their stomach. The belief grew up that these crocodilians attacked people. In fact, these objects are deposited in rivers along with the remains from cremations. The gharials swallow them to aid their digestion and possibly also to help with buoyancy. Most crocodilians simply swallow stones for this purpose.

for a distance of over 372 miles (598 km), providing an important potential refuge for these crocodilians. However, outside India in other parts of their former range there are believed to be fewer than 200 gharials surviving in the wild.

Common name American alligator

Scientific name *Alligator mississippiensis*

Subfamily Alligatorinae

Family Crocodylidae

Order Crocodylia

Size Large specimens measure up to 13 ft (4 m); reports of individuals up to 20 ft (6 m) long are unsubstantiated

Weight Can exceed 550 lb (249 kg)

Key features Body almost black; snout relatively long, wide, and rounded; front feet have 5 toes on each; hind feet have 4; when the mouth is closed, only upper teeth visible (which distinguishes alligators from crocodiles)

Habits Active during the summer; may hibernate during the winter, especially in northern areas; semiaquatic, emerging to bask on land; can move quite fast on land and will search for new habitat when pools dry up

Breeding Female lays clutches of 30–70 eggs; hatchlings emerge after about 2 months

Diet Carnivorous; feeds on prey ranging from crustaceans to much larger aquatic life, including fish, turtles, and wading birds, as well as mammals

Habitat Rivers, marshland, and swamps; sometimes in brackish water; rarely seen at sea

Distribution Southeastern United States from Texas to Florida and north through the Carolinas

Status Delisted from being an endangered species in 1985, having been the subject of a successful recovery program; listed on CITES Appendix II

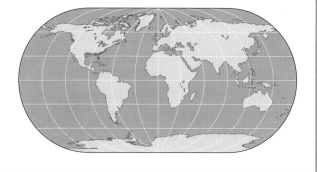

American Alligator

Alligator mississippiensis

Once on the verge of extinction, the American alligator has made a real comeback. Trade in its skin and meat is now strictly controlled, and the alligator has been reinstated as a vital part of the entire ecosystem.

THE AMERICAN ALLIGATOR USED TO range over a much wider area. About half a million years ago it reached as far north as the present-day state of Maryland. Then climatic changes occurred, and its range started to contract. However, when European settlers reached the southeastern area of the country, they found that these reptiles were still very common. Habitat modifications and hunting pressures subsequently reduced their range even more, and American alligators disappeared from the southeastern parts of Virginia and Oklahoma. Today their range includes Mississippi, Arkansas, eastern Texas, the Carolinas, and Alabama, although the species' main strongholds are southern Georgia, Louisiana, and Florida.

The relatively large size of these reptiles has given them a critical role in maintaining the entire ecosystem in which they occur because they dig so-called "gator holes" using their tail and snout. These provide temporary reservoirs of water and therefore maintain suitable aquatic habitats for various other animal and plant life. Vegetation around "gator holes" always tends to be lush thanks to the silt that the alligators deposit on the banks. The movements of alligators on regular paths can also create additional channels that enable water to run into marshlands more easily during periods of heavy rain.

Disguised as Logs

These reptiles often spend long periods floating motionless on the surface of the water, where they resemble partially submerged logs. They lie

SEE ALSO Crocodilians 47:94; Gharial 47:98; Crocodile, Saltwater 47:108

with their nostrils above the water's surface so that they can breathe easily. This behavior allows them to spot and ambush prey and also helps them maintain their body temperature, since they can warm themselves up from the sun without leaving the water. This is achieved by means of the osteoderms, or bone swellings, along the back that are linked with blood vessels. Heat is absorbed into the body there, helped by the alligators' dark coloration, and then circulated through the bloodstream.

A similar method is used by many other crocodilians, but it is especially important in this species because of the relatively temperate areas in which the alligators are found. During the winter they become sluggish. They retreat to the bottom of the waterway or burrow into a riverbank below the waterline and only emerge when the weather is warm. At this time their heart rate can reduce to just one beat per minute. The heart has a complex four-chambered structure more like that of a mammal than a reptile. American alligators can also survive being trapped in ice, provided that their nostrils are not submerged. It has even

⊖ *Almost black in color, the American alligator has prominent eyes and nostrils and coarse scales all over its body. Its upper teeth are visible along the top jaw.*

It Just Takes Two

The only other species of alligator is the smaller Chinese alligator, *A. sinensis*, which reaches a maximum size of approximately 7 feet (2.13 m). It has a very limited area of distribution today in China's Yangtze Valley and is highly endangered, with an overall population of only about 300 individuals. Captive-breeding programs in China and overseas, particularly in the United States, are underway with the aim of creating a more viable population. In terms of its habits this species appears to have a lifestyle similar to that of the American alligator, hibernating in burrows over the winter. The young mature slightly earlier, however, typically at about four years old.

been known for them to recover after over eight hours frozen beneath the water's surface without breathing thanks to their low oxygen requirement under these conditions. Alligators lose their appetite dramatically in the winter, and they are likely to stop eating altogether simply because their slow metabolism does not allow them to digest food at this stage.

Their relatively wide snout allows them to tackle a variety of prey, and the mouth itself contains about 80 teeth. They are constantly replaced throughout the alligator's life as they become worn or even broken, but the rate of growth slows markedly in old age. As a result, older alligators may have difficulty catching prey to the point of facing starvation. Older individuals are more likely to resort to attacking people for this reason, since they often represent a relatively easy target.

Encounters with Humans

With the ability to swim and run over very short distances at speeds of up to 30 mph (48 kph)—significantly faster than a human—American alligators will take a wide variety of prey. Generally they do not pose a major threat to humans. But as they have increased in numbers again over recent years and development has encroached farther into the swamps of Florida, for example, greater conflicts have arisen. They often take the form of an alligator emerging onto the green of a golf course or roaming into a backyard area rather than actual attacks. Unfortunately, chain-link fencing is not an effective barrier, since these alligators can climb fences up to 6 feet (1.8 m) tall without a problem. Those that threaten or harm the public are caught under a nuisance alligator program and may be moved elsewhere.

When attacks on people occur, they are often the result of the reptile being threatened or caught unawares. Feeding alligators is

Mutant Alligators

Two very rare color mutations of the American alligator have been documented. There is a pure albino form, characterized by its reddish eyes and white body. There is also a separate leucistic variant, in which the alligators have an attractive pale yellow body color. They can be further distinguished from the albino form by their blue eyes.

There are an estimated 70 albinos, and many of them are exhibited in zoological collections or breeding farms that are open to the public. This is because their coloration makes them so conspicuous that they would be extremely vulnerable to predators in the wild. Leucistic alligators are even rarer, known from a clutch of just 17 individuals that were discovered in Savoy, Louisiana, in 1987. A single female was then found at a site 100 miles (160 km) away in 1994. Both these mutant forms are also vulnerable to skin cancer because of the lack of protective melanin pigment in their bodies, and so they need to be kept in shaded surroundings.

↑ *Albino American alligators are quite rare. Most of them, including this individual from Los Angeles, are kept in captivity because they would be unable to survive in the wild.*

→ *American alligators will eat anything they can catch. In the Florida Everglades a raccoon is this alligator's next meal.*

especially dangerous, since they soon come to associate people with being a source of food. Children are more vulnerable to attack than adults because of their smaller size, but dogs are especially at risk. Alligators appear to have a particular dislike for them, possibly because they regard their barking as a threat.

American alligators communicate with each other by letting out a roar that can be heard over 1 mile (1.6 km) away. They also make a noise by slapping down their jaw on the water's surface. In addition, they keep in touch with each other by means of vibrations transmitted through the water using their throat and stomach. These sounds are made more frequently in the spring—males call to attract females in their territories, which may extend over an area of up to 10 square miles (26 sq km). They also track each other by means of special scent glands located in the cloaca and on each side of the jaw.

Dry Nesting Sites

The mating period is influenced by locality but typically lasts from March to May, with egg laying occurring a month later. The female will seek out a spot that is unlikely to flood but that is nevertheless located close to the water and often partially concealed among trees and other vegetation. The eggs will not survive in flooded ground and will be ruined if they are immersed for more than 12 hours. The female constructs a nest for her eggs by piling plant matter up to a height of 36 inches (90 cm). As the vegetation rots, it emits heat and warms the eggs, which measure about 3 inches (7.5 cm).

The incubation temperature is critical in determining the gender of the hatchlings. At temperatures below 85°F (29.5°C) the majority of hatchlings will be female, whereas above that figure males will predominate. It will be about two months before the young

⊕ *Although as adults they are among the largest reptiles and can grow up to 13 feet (4 m) long, American alligators are only about 9 inches (23 cm) in length when they hatch.*

alligators emerge from the nest. Their mother hears them uttering their distinctive "yipping" calls and helps them out. She carries them to the water in her mouth, with her tongue serving as a pouch.

The young alligators measure about 9 inches (23 cm) long when they hatch and are much more brightly colored than the adults, with a black-and-yellow banded patterning on their body. They stay together as a group (known as a pod) in close proximity to the female until they are two years old. During this time the mother will try to protect them. A number will be lost, however, sometimes even to large males. Other potential predators include wading birds, gars, and other large fish. By the time they are six years old, the young alligators are likely to have reached about 6.8 feet (2.1 m) in length, after which their growth rate slows significantly.

Alligator Recovery Programs

In the first half of the 20th century American alligators were killed in large numbers. Some estimates suggest that more than 10 million of these reptiles were hunted and killed for their skins between 1870 and 1970. Since that time, however, their numbers have increased dramatically thanks to effective conservation measures based partly on an acknowledgement of the commercial value of the alligators.

There are now over 150 alligator farms in various states, including Louisiana, Florida, and Texas. In the early days especially they helped restore wild populations. Farmers were permitted to remove a percentage of eggs from the nests of wild alligators, which they could hatch artificially, but a significant percentage of the resulting offspring had to be returned to the wild to repopulate areas where the species had disappeared or become very scarce.

An incidental but important benefit of these recovery programs has been our increased knowledge of the biology of the alligators. In turn this has helped develop effective management plans for wild populations. In Florida, for example, it has been shown that the

alligators' reproductive potential is such that eggs could be taken from half of all nests with no adverse effects on the overall population.

Because of better habitat management larger areas are available to alligators and the other creatures living alongside them. There are some new concerns, however, notably about the rising level of mercury in certain alligator populations as a result of industrial pollution. Since the alligators are at the top of the food chain, this contaminant accumulates in their bodies from their prey. Its long-term effects are as yet unclear because, once they have survived the vulnerable stage as hatchlings, alligators can live for at least 50 years and possibly closer to a century in some cases.

This eight-week-old hatchling in the Florida Everglades is vulnerable to predation by larger aquatic animals. Juveniles usually stay in small groups close to their mother for the first two years.

Skin Tagging

Careful monitoring by means of tagging ensures that skins of illegally killed alligators cannot be traded. The success of this program has been shown by the fact that the alligator population in Louisiana has grown today to just below that of a century ago in spite of the massive development that has occurred during this period.

Although the skins are the most valuable items and are exported worldwide (especially to markets in Europe, such as Italy, as well as to

Japan), alligator meat has also acquired something of a gourmet reputation and can be found on the menus of fashionable restaurants in many cities. Even the teeth of these reptiles are in demand and are made into jewelry or simply sold as curios.

⊙ *American alligators often live in close proximity to humans and are an important attraction on the itinerary of many tourists visiting the southeastern states.*

Common name Black caiman

Scientific name *Melanosuchus niger*

Subfamily Alligatorinae

Family Crocodylidae

Order Crocodylia

Size Up 20 ft (6.1 m), making it the largest of all South American crocodilians

Weight Approximately 500 lb (227 kg)

Key features Body black with dots that are especially evident in young hatchlings; head gray in youngsters, becoming reddish-brown as they age; snout relatively wide at the base, rapidly narrowing along its length; an obvious bony ridge is evident above the eyes, continuing down the snout; protective body casing on the neck and back is the thickest of all crocodilians

Habits Nocturnal hunter; often encountered in flooded areas of forest during the wet season

Breeding Female produces clutch of 50–60 eggs that are deposited in a nest mound; eggs hatch after 6 weeks

Diet Young feed on aquatic invertebrates and small fish; larger individuals eat bigger prey, including some mammals

Habitat Shallow areas of water in rain-forest areas

Distribution Confined to the Amazon drainage basin; appears to be conspicuously absent from Surinam

Status Has declined in many parts of its range as the result of heavy hunting for the leather trade during the second half of the 20th century; IUCN Lower Risk; CITES Appendices I and II

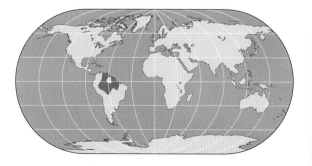

Black Caiman

Melanosuchus niger

In spite of its name, the black caiman is one of the more colorful crocodilians. The white spots on its black body are particularly bright in young hatchlings.

THE HABITS OF THE BLACK CAIMAN appear to be closest to those of the land crocodiles of the past. It is an agile hunter found in shallow stretches of water. It finds its prey by a combination of sight and sound—it has very acute hearing. As they grow larger, the caimans feed on mammals. They sometimes take domestic livestock such as pigs and dogs, but they rarely attack humans. In some areas they have been known to prey regularly on cattle.

The black caiman's relatively large size has made the species an attractive target for hunters, and a huge trade in skins developed out of Colombia from the 1940s onward. About 60,000 hides were exported annually from this country alone right up until the 1970s, and a survey at the end of that decade showed that the species had been virtually wiped out in Colombia. Overall, the total population of black caimans throughout South America is now believed to be just 1 percent of the numbers that existed there a century ago.

Unfortunately, even when given protection, it is difficult for the caiman to recolonize former habitats. This is because it faces competition from the smaller, more adaptable common caiman, *Caiman crocodilus*, which has become more widespread. Common caimans adjust well to habitat changes, they are less conspicuous by nature, and they breed more rapidly. The last remaining stronghold of the black caiman appears to be French Guiana, particularly around Kaw, where the largest surviving examples are most likely to be found today.

Breeding and Lifestyle

The nesting season of black caimans usually begins during the dry season throughout their range. The female constructs a mass of

vegetation that can measure up to 30 inches (76 cm) high and up to 5 feet (1.5 m) across. The siting of the nest varies—sometimes it is hidden farther inside the rain forest than at other times. It is not uncommon for several females to nest in a similar area. The hatchlings then emerge from their eggs after a period of six weeks. Females may become more aggressive when nesting, although not all of them appear to display strong maternal protective instincts—some simply abandon their nests after they have finished laying their eggs.

Black caimans are known to undertake seasonal movements. Early 19th-century naturalists visiting the Amazon first described the way in which these crocodilians preferred the relative shallows of the flooded forests during the wet season, only returning to the main river channels during the dry season when the water level was much lower. In some parts of the lower Amazon where river flow can fall dramatically, they would even estivate by burrowing into mud, while large numbers congregated in remaining areas of water.

Hunting of the caimans was common at that time of the year, notably around Marajó Island. The island is located at the mouth of the Amazon, and cattle ranchers there were desperate to protect their stock from attacks by these crocodilians.

⊕ *A butterfly seems unaware of the potential danger from the powerful jaws of this black caiman basking on a log in Peru.*

Unusual Fishing Technique

Fish figure prominently in the diet of the black caiman, with larger individuals hunting the big freshwater catfish found in the waters of the Amazon basin. Black caimans have developed a very efficient way of catching and stunning fish, using movements of their powerful tail. They advance quietly toward their target. They lash out with the tail; then almost imperceptibly, using the tail like a hand, they bring the fish around to their mouth. They hunt at night, and the distinctive smacking sound made by the caiman's tail on the surface of the water indicates that these crocodilians are present in the area.

Common name Saltwater crocodile (Indo-Pacific crocodile, estuarine crocodile)

Scientific name *Crocodylus porosus*

Subfamily Crocodylinae

Family Crocodylidae

Order Crocodylia

Size At least 23 feet (7 m) long; possibly up to 30 feet (9 m), but this is unconfirmed

Weight Possibly in excess of 2,418 lb (1,097 kg)

Key features Broad, powerful snout and strong jaws; a ridge runs from each eye toward the center of the snout; usually quite light in color when adult with overall gray or tan coloration; darker banding may be apparent on the tail with the smooth underparts creamy yellow; young are more colorful with clearer contrast between light and dark areas; has less bony protection on the head shield than any other living species of crocodile

Habits Highly aggressive predator; powerful swimmer; diurnal

Breeding Female lays 1 clutch of 60–80 eggs and guards them until they hatch after about 3 months

Diet Hatchlings prey on small aquatic animals; adults eat larger prey ranging from buffalo to sharks

Habitat Found in a variety of environments from rivers, lakes, and swamps to the open ocean

Distribution Eastern India, Southeast Asia, Papua New Guinea, Australia, and other Pacific islands

Status Relatively common; numbers have increased in some areas thanks to protective measures; IUCN Lower Risk; CITES Appendices I and II

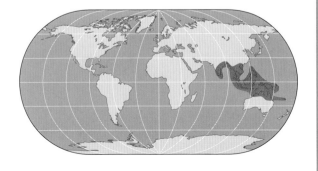

Saltwater Crocodile

Crocodylus porosus

The largest and most feared crocodile in the world, the saltwater crocodile is a confirmed man-eater, thought to kill as many as 1,000 people each year. Just like sharks, these crocodiles have acquired a gruesome reputation for congregating at the site of disasters, such as boating accidents, and preying on survivors.

THE SALTWATER CROCODILE is the most widely distributed of today's crocodilians. Its ability to travel long distances across the Pacific has enabled it to colonize islands far from the Asian mainland. Saltwater crocodiles have even been seen farther north in the vicinity of Japan. Recent research has also shown that the crocodiles on the Seychelles that went extinct in the 1800s belonged to this species rather than the Nile crocodile, *Crocodylus niloticus*, as previously thought. Some saltwater crocodiles that have been found even have well-established barnacles on their backs, indicating that they must have spent a considerable amount of time in the marine environment.

During the second half of the 20th century populations of saltwater crocodiles plummeted because large numbers were slaughtered for their skins, which are regarded as the most valuable of all crocodilian skins in terms of commercial trade. Wildlife management programs, especially in Australia, have since seen a resurgence in crocodile numbers, however. In addition, farming of these reptiles has resulted in a more sustainable trade.

Breeding

Courtship in saltwater crocodiles can be aggressive, and the males often fight among themselves in the breeding season. During

⊙ *In the Adelaide River in South Australia a saltwater crocodile rears up out of the water as food is offered. Adults eat anything they can find, even large mammals.*

 SEE ALSO Monitor Lizards **46**:82; Crocodilians **47**:94; Crocodile, Nile **47**:110

mating the male holds the female with his forelegs placed on either side of her neck. Males are sexually mature by the time they are about 16 years old, once they have grown to approximately 10.3 feet (3.2 m). Females start to lay at a smaller size, once they are about 7.2 feet (2.2 m) long and about 10 years old. They build a large nest mound for their eggs and guard the site diligently against potential predators such as monitor lizards, *Varanus* species, throughout the incubation period. They remain nearby for almost three months.

The female digs her eggs out of the nest once they are ready to hatch and carries the young hatchlings in her mouth to the safety of the water. At first, the young remain together in groups known as pods. Over half of them will die during their first year, a time when they are at their most vulnerable to predators because of their size. Young saltwater crocodiles can even fall prey to Australia's other crocodilian species, Johnston's crocodile, *C. johnstoni*, or be eaten by large snake-necked turtles, *Chelodina* species.

Attacks on Boats

Saltwater crocodiles sometimes exhibit strange behavior. Some large individuals regularly attack small boats, even persisting in damaging the craft when its occupants have been forced into the water. A particularly famous case of this kind involved a saltwater crocodile in Australia's Northern Territory, which became known as "Sweetheart." This individual is believed to have been responsible for a series of attacks that began in 1974 and only ceased after its capture in July 1979. This giant was found to measure 17 feet (5.2 m) long.

Although the propeller of the outboard motor was the usual target for the crocodile's attacks, Sweetheart actually bit directly through the aluminum hull of one boat. Luckily, although no one was hurt during these incidents, Sweetheart died soon after being caught, probably as a result of stress. It is now believed that the shape of the outboard motor seen from under the water and its resultant noise are confused by these reptiles with a rival crocodile entering their territory. Therefore they attack. This explains why it was only the boats (especially the motor, which is seen as the "head" of the invading crocodile) and not the people that were targeted by Sweetheart.

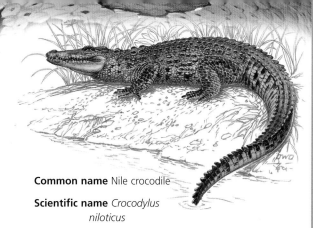

Common name Nile crocodile

Scientific name *Crocodylus niloticus*

Subfamily Crocodylinae

Family Crocodylidae

Order Crocodylia

Size Largest official record is 19.5 ft (6 m) from snout to tail; large specimens today are usually no longer than 16 ft (4.9 m)

Weight Up to 2,300 lb (1,043 kg)

Key features Appearance variable, leading to the identification of numerous subspecies; body usually dark, sometimes blackish, with lighter underparts; young are olive-brown with blackish markings across the body; mouthparts broad and powerful

Habits Large individuals are aggressive and dangerous, seizing prey at the water's edge; uses speed and stealth for hunting; diurnal; sometimes bask on shore

Breeding Female usually lays 16–80 eggs in a clutch depending on age and subspecies; nest guarding known in both sexes; eggs hatch after about 2 months

Diet Young hatchlings feed largely on aquatic creatures, including invertebrates and amphibians; adults take much larger prey, including giraffes and even humans

Habitat Usually restricted to freshwater habitats; may be found on beaches and occasionally at sea

Distribution Africa, occurring over a very wide area south and east of the Sahara; also found on the island of Zanzibar

Status Some decline in local populations but relatively common overall; listed on CITES Appendices I and II

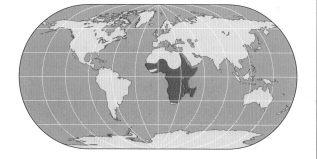

Nile Crocodile

Crocodylus niloticus

Nile crocodiles occur all over Africa, eating almost anything but rarely moving away from their favorite body of water. They are the largest African crocodiles, and their reputation as man-eaters is justified.

NILE CROCODILES ARE THOUGHT to kill about 300 people annually in Africa. The species has proved to be highly adaptable, and its population has withstood heavy hunting for over a century. The leather trade accounted for the deaths of over three million Nile crocodiles in just 30 years until 1980.

Crocodile Ranches

A ranching program at Lake Kariba, Zimbabwe, benefits from the high reproductive potential of these reptiles. Ranching entails taking a small percentage of the eggs laid by wild crocodiles under permit, hatching them artificially, and rearing the offspring in captivity. A crucial aspect of the program (which has become a model for others) is that some of the young crocodiles must be released back to the wild. When ranching began, Nile crocodiles were on the verge of extinction in Zimbabwe, but the current wild population has grown to over 50,000 individuals. The only significant drawback is that there have been an increased number of crocodile attacks on humans again.

The actual farming of crocodiles (in which breeding stock is retained on site and the eggs hatched there) began in Zimbabwe once the success of ranching became apparent. A unique, tamperproof tagging system has been developed to ensure that crocodile skins entering international trade can be monitored by the authorities, eliminating the risk of any illegal killing.

In the wild young hatchling crocodiles are shy. They remain in the shallows, feeding mainly on aquatic prey including amphibians, but they have a well-developed social structure. By two years old, when they are approaching 3.3 feet

⊕ *Nile crocodiles may bask on shore before sliding into the water to protect themselves from the midday sun, opening their mouth in a wide yawn to allow heat to escape.*

(1 m) in length, they start associating with each other in deeper water. After this stage they seek to join existing adult groups, but they are not always welcomed by the dominant bull (male). If challenged by a larger group member, a young Nile crocodile will raise its head out of the water in a submissive gesture. It will then retreat below the water again without any fighting taking place.

In spite of their reputation as Africa's most lethal aquatic predators, Nile crocodiles can occasionally come off worse in attacks, especially when elephants are involved. In one case the elephant responded by pulling the crocodile out of the water while it was still gripping onto the elephant's leg. Another member of the herd then trampled the unfortunate reptile to death, whereupon the elephant that had been attacked picked up the crocodile's body with its trunk and hurled it up into a tree. Similar behavior has been observed on more than one occasion.

Grooming Associates

One of the more remarkable aspects of the behavior of the Nile crocodiles is the way in which they allow certain birds (notably spur-winged plovers, *Vanellus spinosus*) to feed on scraps of food that attach to their teeth and also to remove parasites such as leeches from their bodies with impunity. This type of grooming by a species that would normally be considered to be prey is not restricted to crocodiles, however. It has also been documented in various communities of reef fish.

Evidence suggests that Nile crocodiles can become easily conditioned to eat humans. A particularly gruesome case occurred on the Zambezi River at a town called Sesheke. The local ruler, King Sepopo, disposed of his enemies by feeding them to the crocodiles; although the practice stopped with his murder in 1870, the crocodile population kept their reputation as man-eaters for decades after his death. This is perhaps not surprising, since the reptiles themselves can live for over 70 years.

Glossary

Words in SMALL CAPITALS refer to other entries in the glossary.

Acrodont (teeth) teeth attached to the upper edge of the jaw, as opposed to the inside surface (PLEURODONT) or in sockets (THECODONT)

Adaptation a characteristic shape, behavior, or physiological process that equips an organism (or group of related organisms) for its way of life and habitat

Advanced relatively recently evolved (opposite of "primitive")

Albino an animal that has no color pigment in its body and has red eyes

Amniotic egg an egg with a fluid-filled sac within a membrane that encloses the embryo of reptiles, birds, and mammals. Animals that produce amniotic eggs are known as amniotes

Amplexus the position adopted during mating in most frogs and many salamanders, in which the male clasps the female with one or both pairs of limbs. See AXILLARY AMPLEXUS and INGUINAL AMPLEXUS

Annuli the growth rings often visible on the shell of CHELONIANS

Anterior the front part or head and shoulders of an animal

Aposematic coloration bright coloration serving to warn a potential predator that an animal is distasteful or poisonous

Arboreal living in trees or shrubs

Autotomy self-amputation of part of the body. Some lizards practice CAUDAL autotomy: They discard all or part of their tail

Axillary amplexus mating position in frogs in which the male grasps the female behind her front limbs. See INGUINAL AMPLEXUS

Barbel a small, elongated "feeler," or sensory process, on the head, usually of aquatic animals, e.g., some pipid frogs

Binocular vision the ability to focus both eyes on a single subject. The eyes must point forward (not sideways as in most reptiles and amphibians). Binocular vision enables animals, including humans, to judge distances

Bridges the sides of a turtle's shell, attaching to the CARAPACE above and the PLASTRON below

Brille the transparent covering over the eyes of snakes and some lizards, such as geckos

Bromeliad member of a family of plants restricted to the New World. Many live attached to trees, including "urn plants" in which ARBOREAL frogs sometimes breed

Calcareous containing calcium carbonate

Carapace the upper part of the shell of turtles and tortoises, the other parts being the PLASTRON and the BRIDGES. Also used to describe the hard structure covering part of any animal's body

Caudal relating to the tail, as in subcaudal scales beneath a snake's tail and caudal (tail) fin

Chelonian a member of the ORDER Chelonia, containing all reptiles variously known as terrapins, turtles, and tortoises

Chromatophore a specialized cell containing pigment, usually located in the outer layers of the skin

Chromosome a thread-shaped structure consisting largely of genetic material (DNA), found in the nucleus of cells

Cirrus (pl. cirri) a slender, usually flexible appendage on an animal

CITES an international conservation organization: Convention on International Trade in Endangered Species

Class a TAXONOMIC category ranking below PHYLUM, containing a number of ORDERS

Cloaca the common chamber into which the urinary, digestive, and reproductive systems discharge their contents, and which opens to the exterior; from Latin meaning "sewer" or "drain"

Clutch the eggs laid by a female at one time

Continuous breeder an animal that may breed at any time of year

Convergent evolution the effect of unrelated animals looking like each other because they have adapted to similar conditions in similar ways

Coprophagy the practice of eating excrement

Costal relating to the ribs

Costal grooves grooves or folds along the flanks of caecilians and some salamanders that correspond to the position of the ribs

Crocodilian a member of the order Crocodylia, including alligators, caimans, crocodiles, and gharials

Cryptic having the ability to remain hidden, usually by means of camouflage, e.g., cryptic coloration

Cutaneous respiration breathing that takes place across the skin's surface, especially important in amphibians

Cycloid disklike, resembling a circle

Denticle toothlike scale

Dermis layer of skin immediately below the EPIDERMIS

Dewlap flap or fold of skin under an animal's throat. Sometimes used in displays, e.g., in anole lizards

Dimorphism the existence of two distinct forms within a SPECIES, which is then said to be dimorphic. In species in which there are more than two forms, they are polymorphic. See SEXUAL DIMORPHISM

Direct development transition from egg to the adult form in amphibians without passing through a free-living LARVAL stage

Dorsal relating to the back or upper surface of the body or one of its parts

Ectotherm (adj. ectothermic) an animal that relies on external heat sources, such as the sun, to raise its body temperature. Reptiles and amphibians are ectotherms. See ENDOTHERM

Eft juvenile, TERRESTRIAL phase in the life cycle of a newt. The red eft is the terrestrial juvenile form of the eastern newt, *Notophthalmus viridescens*

Egg tooth small toothlike scale that some amphibians and reptiles have on the tip of the snout to assist in breaking through their eggshell

Endemic SPECIES, GENERA, or FAMILIES that are restricted to a particular geographical region

Endotherm (adj. endothermic) an animal that can sustain a high body temperature by means of heat generated within the body by the metabolism. See ECTOTHERM

Epidermis surface layer of the skin of a vertebrate

Epiphyte plant growing on another plant but not a parasite. Includes many orchids and BROMELIADS and some mosses and ferns

Estivation a state of inactivity during prolonged periods of drought or high temperature. During estivation the animal often buries itself in soil or mud. See HIBERNATION

Estuarine living in the lower part of a river (estuary) where fresh water meets and mixes with seawater

Explosive breeder a SPECIES in which the breeding season is very short, resulting in large numbers of animals mating at the same time

External fertilization fusing of eggs and sperm outside the female's body, as in nearly all frogs and toads. See INTERNAL FERTILIZATION

Family TAXONOMIC category ranking below ORDER, containing GENERA that are more closely related to one another than any other grouping of genera

Farming hatching and rearing of young CHELONIANS and CROCODILIANS from a captive-breeding population. See RANCHING

Fauna the animal life of a locality or region

Femoral gland gland situated on an animal's thigh

Femoral pores row of pores along an animal's thighs. Most obvious in many lizards

Fertilization union of an egg and a sperm

Gamete OVUM or sperm

Genus (pl. genera) taxonomic category ranking below FAMILY; a group of SPECIES all more closely related to one another than to any other group of species

Gestation carrying the developing young within the body. Gestation period is the length of time that this occurs

Gill respiratory structure in aquatic animals through which gas exchange takes place

Gill slits slits in which GILLS are situated and present in some amphibians and their LARVAE

Granular (scale) small grainlike scales covering the body, as in some geckos and in the file snakes, *Acrochordus*

Gravid carrying eggs or young

Gular pouch area of expandable skin in the throat region

Hedonic glands glands in a male salamander that stimulate a female when they are rubbed against her body

Heliotherm an animal that basks to regulate body temperature

Hemipenis (pl. hemipenes) one of two grooved copulatory structures present in the males of some reptiles

Herbivore animal that eats plants

Heterogeneous (scales) scales that differ in shape or size. See HOMOGENEOUS (SCALES)

Hibernation a period of inactivity, often spent underground, to avoid extremes of cold. See ESTIVATION

Hinge a means by which the PLASTRON of some CHELONIANS can be pulled up, giving the reptile more protection against a would-be predator

Home range an area in which an animal lives except for MIGRATIONS or rare excursions

Homogeneous (scales) scales that are all the same shape and size. See HETEROGENEOUS (SCALES)

Hyoid "u"-shaped bone at the base of the tongue to which the larynx is attached

Inguinal pertaining to the groin

Inguinal amplexus a mating position in which a male frog or salamander clasps a female around the lower abdomen. See AXILLARY AMPLEXUS

Intergular scute a single plate, or SCUTE, lying between the paired gular scutes on the PLASTRON of side-necked turtles

Internal fertilization fusing of eggs and sperm inside the female's body, as in reptiles and most salamanders. See EXTERNAL FERTILIZATION

Interstitial the thin skin between the scales of reptiles. Sometimes called "interscalar" skin

Introduced species brought from lands where it occurs naturally to lands where it has not previously occurred

IUCN International Union for the Conservation of Nature, responsible for assigning animals and plants to internationally agreed categories of rarity. *See* table below

Jacobson's organ (or vomeronasal organ) one of a pair of grooves extending from the nasal cavity and opening into the mouth cavity in some mammals and reptiles. Molecules collected on the tongue are sampled by this organ, which supplements the sense of smell

Juvenile young animal, not sexually mature

Karst a porous form of limestone

Keeled scales a ridge on the DORSAL scales of some snakes

Keratophagy the practice of eating molted skin

Lamella (pl. lamellae) thin transverse plates across the undersides of the toes of some lizards, especially geckos

Larva (pl. larvae) early stage in the development of an animal (including amphibians) after hatching from the egg

Lateral line organ sense organ embedded in the skin of some aquatic animals, including LARVAL salamanders and some frogs, which responds to waterborne vibrations. Usually arranged in a row along the animal's side

Leucistic an animal that lacks all pigment except that in its eyes. Partially leucistic animals have patches of white over an otherwise normally pigmented skin. See ALBINO

Life cycle complete life history of an organism from one stage to the recurrence of that stage, e.g., egg to egg

Life history history of a single individual organism from the fertilization of the egg until its death

Lifestyle general mode of life of an animal, e.g., NOCTURNAL predator, aquatic HERBIVORE, parasite

Live-bearing giving birth to young that have developed beyond the egg stage. Live-bearers may be VIVIPAROUS or OVOVIVIPAROUS

Lure (noun) part of the body, such as the tail, that is used to entice prey closer

Mental gland gland on the chin of some newts and salamanders that appears to stimulate the female during courtship; one of the HEDONIC GLANDS

Metabolism chemical or energy changes occurring within a living organism that are involved in various life activities

Metamorphosis transformation of an animal from one stage of its life history to another, e.g., from LARVA to adult

Microenvironment local conditions that immediately surround an organism

Migration movement of animals from one place to another, often in large numbers and often for breeding purposes

Mimic an animal that resembles an animal belonging to another SPECIES, usually a distasteful or venomous one, or some inedible object

Milt sperm-containing fluid produced by a male frog during egg laying to fertilize the eggs

Montane pertaining to mountains or SPECIES that live in mountains

Morph form or phase of an animal

Morphological relating to the form and structure of an organism

Nasolabial groove a groove running from the nostril to the upper lip in male plethodontid salamanders

Neonate the newborn young of a live-bearer

Neoteny condition in which a LARVA fails to METAMORPHOSE and retains its larval features as an adult. Species with this condition are said to be neotenic. The axolotl is the best-known example. See PEDOMORPHOSIS

Neotropics the tropical part of the New World, including northern South America, Central America, part of Mexico, and the West Indies

Newt amphibious salamanders of the genera *Triturus, Taricha,* and *Notophthalmus*

Niche the role played by a SPECIES in its particular community. It is determined by its food and temperature preferences; each species' niche within a community is unique

Nocturnal active at night

Nuptial pad an area of dark, rough skin that develops in male amphibians on the hands, arms, or chest of some SPECIES prior to the breeding season. Its purpose is to allow the male to grip the female in AMPLEXUS

Occipital lobe the pyramid-shaped area at the back of the brain that helps an animal interpret vision

Ocular of the eye

Olfactory relating to the sense of smell

Omnivore an animal that eats both animal and plant material

Order taxonomic category ranking below CLASS and above FAMILY

Osteoderm small bone in the skin of some reptiles; lies under the scales

Ovary female gonad or reproductive organ that produces the OVUM

Overwinter survive the winter

Oviduct the duct in females that carries the OVUM from the ovary to the CLOACA

Oviparous reproducing by eggs that hatch outside the female's body

IUCN CATEGORIES

EX **Extinct,** when there is no reasonable doubt that the last individual of the species has died.

EW **Extinct in the Wild,** when a species is known only to survive in captivity or as a naturalized population well outside the past range.

CR **Critically Endangered,** when a species is facing an extremely high risk of extinction in the wild in the immediate future.

EN **Endangered,** when a species is facing a very high risk of extinction in the wild in the near future.

VU **Vulnerable,** when a species is facing a high risk of extinction in the wild in the medium-term future.

LR **Lower Risk,** when a species has been evaluated and does not satisfy the criteria for CR, EN, or VU.

DD **Data Deficient,** when there is not enough information about a species to assess the risk of extinction.

NE **Not Evaluated,** species that have not been assessed by the IUCN criteria.

Ovoviviparous reproducing by eggs that the female retains within her body until they hatch; the developing eggs contain a yolk sac but receive no nourishment from the mother through a placenta or similar structure

Ovum (pl. ova) female germ cell or GAMETE; an egg cell or egg

Papilla (pl. papillae) aised projection(s) of soft tissue often seen on the head and neck of aquatic CHELONIANS

Parietal eye a VESTIGIAL eye situated in the top of the head of tuataras and some lizards, sometimes known as the "third eye"

Parietals pairs of bones forming the rear of the roof of the brain case

Parotid glands pair of large glands on the shoulder, neck, or behind the eye in some salamanders and toads

Parthenogenesis a form of asexual reproduction in which the OVUM develops without being fertilized. Such SPECIES are said to be parthenogenetic

Parturition the process of giving birth to live young

Pectoral girdle the skeleton supporting the forelimbs of a land vertebrate

Pedogenesis form of reproduction by an animal still showing LARVAL characteristics

Pedomorphosis the retention of immature or LARVAL characteristics, such as GILLS, by animals that are sexually mature. See NEOTENY

Permeable property of a substance, such as skin, allowing another substance, such as water, to pass through it

Pheromone a substance released by an organism to induce a response in another individual of the same SPECIES, such as sexual attraction

Phylum taxonomic category ranking above CLASS and below kingdom

Pigment a substance that gives color to part or all of an organism's body

Plastron the ventral portion, or underside, of the shell of a turtle

Pleurodont teeth teeth that are attached to the inside surface of the jaw, as opposed to the upper edge (ACRODONT) or in sockets (THECODONT)

Pond-type larva salamander LARVA with high fins and a deep body, adapted to living in still water. See STREAM-TYPE LARVA

Preanal pores chemical- or pheromone-secreting pores in front of the CLOACA, usually in lizards

Prehensile adapted for grasping or clasping, especially by wrapping around, such as the tail of chameleons

Preocular relating to the front of the eye

Ranching artificial incubation of eggs collected from the wild followed by captive-rearing of the young. A method used with both CHELONIANS and CROCODILIANS to increase population numbers, carried out in an environment free from predators

Rectilinear locomotion a form of movement used by heavy-bodied snakes in which the body progresses in a straight line

Riffle agitated water flowing over rocks or gravel in shallow streams or rivers

Rostral processes extensions to the snout, including horns and other ornamentation

Salt glands glands located in the vicinity of the eye that allow marine turtles and some CROCODILIANS to excrete excessive salt from their bodies, helping prevent them from becoming dehydrated in the marine environment

Satellite male a male frog that does not call but sits near a calling male and intercepts females attracted to the calling male

Savanna open grasslands with scattered trees and bushes, usually in warm areas

Scute enlarged scale on a reptile, including the colorful scales that cover the shell of turtles; divided into different groups, such as the vertebral scutes that run above the VERTEBRAL COLUMN

Sexual dimorphism the existence of marked morphological differences between males and females

Species taxonomic category ranking below GENUS; a group of organisms with common attributes capable of interbreeding and producing healthy fertile offspring

Spermatheca a pouch or sac in the female reproductive tract in which sperm are stored

Spermatophore a structure containing sperm that is passed from the male to the female in some animals, such as in many salamanders

Stream-type larva streamlined LARVA with low fins and elongated body, adapted for living in flowing water. See POND-TYPE LARVA

Subcaudal beneath the tail, as in "subcaudal" scales. See CAUDAL

Subocular usually refers to scales below the eye. See PREOCULAR

Subspecies a locally distinct group of animals that differ slightly from the normal appearance of the SPECIES; often called a race

Substrate the solid material on which an organism lives, e.g., sand, mud, etc.

Suture the zigzag patterning formed beneath the SCUTES where the bones of a CHELONIAN's shell fuse together

Tadpole LARVAL stage of a frog or toad

Talus slopes slopes covered with loose rocks and slabs. Also known as scree

Taxonomy the science of classification: the arrangement of animals and plants into groups based on their natural relationships

Temporal relating to the area between the eye and ear

Terrestrial living on land

Territorial defending an area so as to exclude other members of the same SPECIES

Territory an area that one or more animals defends against other members of the same SPECIES

Thecodont teeth growing in sockets. See ACRODONT

Thermoregulate to expose to or move away from a heat source in order to maintain desired body temperature

Thermoregulation control of body temperature by behavioral or physiological means, so that it maintains a constant or near-constant value

Thyroid gland a gland lying in the neck that produces the hormone THYROXINE

Thyroxine a hormone containing iodine that is involved in a variety of physiological processes, including METAMORPHOSIS in amphibians

Toad any stout-bodied, warty-skinned frog, especially one living away from water. The term has no TAXONOMIC basis, although members of the FAMILY Bufonidae are often called toads

Tongue-flicking constant use of the tongue by snakes and some lizards when exploring their surroundings. Used in conjunction with JACOBSON'S ORGAN

Tubercle a small, knoblike projection

Turtle any shelled reptile, including tortoises and terrapins

Tympanum (pl. tympana) eardrum

Unisexual species a SPECIES consisting only of females, in which reproduction is by PARTHENOGENESIS

Unken reflex a defensive posture shown by some amphibians when attacked, in which the body is arched inward with the head and tail lifted upward. Its purpose is to display a brightly colored underside

Uterine milk a uterine secretion that provides developing embryos with nourishment

Vent the CLOACAL opening of the body. Measurements of reptiles and amphibians are often given as "snout-vent" lengths or simply "s-v" lengths

Ventral describing the lower surface of the body or one of its parts

Vertebral column the spinal skeleton, or backbone, consisting of a series of vertebrae extending from the skull to the tip of the tail

Vertebrate a member of the subphylum Vertebrata, comprising all animals with a VERTEBRAL COLUMN, including fish, amphibians, reptiles, birds, and mammals

Vestigial smaller and of more simple structure than in an evolutionary ancestor. In reptiles and amphibians often used to describe limbs that have become reduced in size through the evolutionary process

Viviparous giving birth to living young that develop within and are nourished by the mother. Often used incorrectly, however, to describe any live-bearing species. See also OVOVIVIPAROUS

Volar pores pores on the underside of the feet

Webbing folds of skin present between the toes of both CROCODILIANS and aquatic CHELONIANS

Xeric adapted to life in an extremely dry habitat

Yolk sac a large sac containing stored nutrients, present in the embryos of fish, amphibians, reptiles, and birds

Further Reading

General

Arnold, E. N., *A Field Guide to the Reptiles and Amphibians of Britain and Europe*, Harper Collins, London, 2002

Behler, J. L., and King, F. W., *The Audubon Society Field Guide to North American Reptiles and Amphibians*, Alfred A. Knopf, New York, 1979

Cogger, H. G., *Reptiles and Amphibians of Australia*, 6th edn., Reed New Holland, Sydney, 2000

Glaw, F., and Vences, M., *A Field Guide to the Reptiles and Amphibians of Madagascar*, 2nd edn., published by the authors, Bonn, 1994

Grismer, L. L., *Amphibians and Reptiles of Baja California*, University of California Press, Berkeley, CA, 2002

Halliday, T., and Adler, C. (eds.), *The New Encyclopedia of Reptiles and Amphibians,* Firefly Books, New York and Toronto/Oxford University Press, Oxford, 2002

Murphy, J. B., Adler, K., and Collins, J. T. (eds.), *Captive Management and Conservation of Reptiles and Amphibians*, Society for the Study of Amphibians and Reptiles, Ithaca, New York, 1994

Savage, J. M., *Amphibians and Reptiles of Costa Rica*, University of Chicago Press, Chicago, 2002

Schleich, H. H., Kästle, W., and Kabisch, K., *Amphibians and Reptiles of North Africa*, Koeltz Scientific Books, Koenigstien, 1996

Zug, G. R., Vitt, L. J., and Caldwell, J. P., *Herpetology: An Introductory Biology of Reptiles and Amphibians*, 2nd edn., Academic Press, San Diego, 2001

Specific to this volume

Alderton, D., *Turtles & Tortoises of the World*, Facts on File, New York, 2003

Alderton, D., *Crocodiles and Alligators of the World*, Facts on File, New York, 2004

Bonin, F., Devaux, B., and Dupré, A., *Toutes les Tortues du Monde*, Delachaux et Niestlé, Lausanne, 1998

Cann, J., *Australian Freshwater Turtles*, John Cann & Beaumont Publishing Pte Ltd, Singapore, 1998

Dijk, P. P. van, Stuart, B. L., & Rhodin, A. C. J. (eds.), *Asian Turtle Trade*, Chelonian Research Foundation, Lunenburg, 2000

Dodd, C. K., *North American Box Turtles: A Natural History*, University of Oklahoma Press, Norman, OK, 2001

Ernst, C.H., and Barbour, R.W., *Turtles of the United States*, The University Press of Kentucky, Lexington, 1972

Ernst, C.H., and Barbour, R.W., *Turtles of the World*, Smithsonian Institution, Washington DC, 1989

Ferri, V., *Turtles & Tortoises*, Firefly Books, New York, 2002

Guggisberg, C.A.W., *Crocodiles: Their Natural History, Folklore and Conservation*, David & Charles, Newton Abbot, 1972

Harless, M, & Morlock, H. (eds.), *Turtles: Perspectives & Research*, Wiley, NY, 1979

Klemens, M. W. (ed.), *Turtle Conservation*, Smithsonian Institution Press, Washington DC, 2000

Orenstein, R., *Survivors in Armor: Turtles, Tortoises and Terrapins*, Key Porter, Toronto, 2001

Pritchard, P. C. H., & Trebbau, P., *The Turtles of Venezuela*, Society for the Study of Amphibians and Reptiles, New York, 1984

Ross, C.A. (ed.), *Crocodiles and Alligators*, Merehurst Press, London, 1989

Steel, R., *Crocodiles*, Christopher Helm, Bromley, 1989

Tikader, B.K., & Sharma, R.C., *Handbook of Indian Testudines*, Zoological Survey of India, Calcutta, 1985

Webb, G. J. W., and Manolis, S.C., *Crocodiles of Australia*, Reed Books, Frenchs Forest, 1989

Zappalorti, R. T., *The Amateur Zoologist's Guide to Turtles and Crocodilians*, Stackpole Books, Harrisburg, 1976

Useful Websites

General

Myers, P. 2001. "Vertebrata" (Online), Animal Diversity. Accessible at:
http://animaldiversity.ummz.umich.edu/site/accounts/information/Amphibia.html

http://www.herplit.com/
A listing of herpetological literature, including older material

http://www.kingsnake.com
Many pages about reptiles and amphibians, especially their care in captivity, and links to other organizations

http://research.amnh.org/herpetology/amphibia/index.html
"Amphibian Species of the World." A catalogue of all amphibian species with synonyms and additional information, accessed with a good search engine

http://www.redlist.org
IUCN Red List gives details of all threatened animals, including reptiles and amphibians

http://www.si.edu/resource/faq/nmnh/zoology.htm#vz
General information about reptiles and amphibians and links to many educational sites

http://tolweb.org/tree?group=Amniota&contgroup=Terrestrial_Vertebrates
A collaborative Internet project produced by biologists from around the world, containing information about the diversity of organisms on earth, their history, and characteristics. All vertebrates are covered. The link given takes you straight to amphibians

Specific to this volume

http://www.cccturtle.org/ccctmp.htm
A good site focusing largely on turtles in the Caribbean, including ongoing satellite tracking of particular individuals

http://www.chelonia.org/
Plenty of information and many links about tortoises and freshwater turtles

http://www.flmnh.ufl.edu/natsci/herpetology/act-plan/plan1998a.htm
Survey of all the world's surviving crocodilians and an action plan to assist their continued survival

http://www.flmnh.ufl.edu/natsci/herpetology/brittoncrocs/csp_amis.htm
Information on the American alligator and other crocodilians of the world

http://www.seaturtle.org/
Another very useful and active sea turtle conservation site

Set Index

A **bold** number shows the volume and is followed by the relevant page numbers (e.g., **21:** 52, 74).

Common names in **bold** (e.g., **adder**) mean that the animal has an illustrated main entry in the set. Underlined page numbers (e.g., **29:** 78–79) refer to the main entry for that animal.

Italic page numbers (e.g., **22:** *103*) point to illustrations of animals in parts of the set other than the main entry.

Page numbers in parentheses—e.g., **21:** (24)—locate information in At-a-Glance boxes.

Animals that have main entries in the set are indexed under their common names, alternative common names, and scientific names.

Picture Credits